W9-BVI-013

THE GOSPEL, THE CHURCH AND THE WORLD

SUBJECTS OF THE COMMISSIONS

Volume I, Commission I-A

The Challenge of Our Culture

What are the main features of the cultures of the world which challenge the Church and its Gospel, and what is the nature of the challenge? Clarence Tucker Craig, *Chairman*

Volume II, Commission I-B

The Church and Organized Movements

What are the allied and opposed organized movements of our day with which the Church must deal? Randolph Crump Miller, *Chairman*

Volume III, Commission II

The Gospel, the Church and the World

What are the resources and limiting factors of the life and Gospel of the Church as it faces the challenge of its world task? Kenneth Scott Latourette, *Chairman*

Volume IV, Commission III

Toward World-Wide Christianity

The Church and the churches. What are the realities and possibilities of ecumenical Christianity? O. Frederick Nolde, *Chairman*

Volume V

What Must the Church Do?

An interpretive volume, presenting the challenge to the Church growing out of the preceding studies. Henry P. Van Dusen

The full membership of the Commissions is given at the end of the volume.

The GOSPEL, *the* CHURCH *and* *the* WORLD

KENNETH SCOTT LATOURETTE
Editor

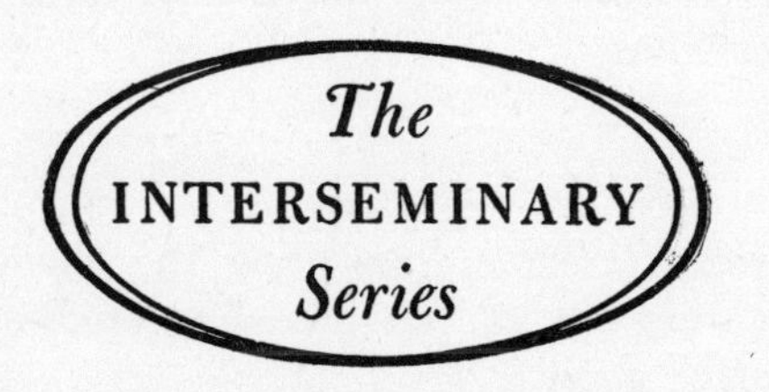

VOLUME THREE

HARPER & BROTHERS · PUBLISHERS
New York and London

THE GOSPEL, THE CHURCH
AND THE WORLD

E-Y

CONTENTS

PREFACE

THE INTERSEMINARY SERIES

The five volumes which comprise "The Interseminary Series" have three main purposes: to outline the character of the contemporary world which challenges the Church; to proclaim afresh the nature of the Gospel and the Church which must meet that challenge; and to set forth the claims which ecumenical Christianity makes upon the various churches as they face their world task. Although the perspective of the volumes is American, it is nevertheless comprehensive in that it views the Church as the Body of Christ in the world, performing a mission to the whole world.

The immediate occasion for the publication of the series is a national conference of theological students scheduled for June, 1947, under the auspices and initiative of the Interseminary Movement in the United States. The volumes will serve as study material for the delegates to the conference.

From the outset, however, it has been the desire and aim of those sponsoring the project that the volumes might have a wide appeal. They have been designed for the Christian public in general, in the hope that there may be in them help toward our common Christian task in the fateful postwar days.

To produce the volumes, the Interseminary Committee outlined the five major questions and organized the Commissions listed at the end of this volume. Each Commission met once, and in the course of a two-day meeting outlined, first, the chapters for its respective volume, and, second, the main elements to be contained in each chapter. Authors were assigned from within the Commission. A first draft of each paper was submitted to Commission members and the chairman of the Commission for criticism, returned and subsequently rewritten in final form. The fifth volume, which is a summary interpretation of the preceding statements, is written by a single author. It should be specially noted that the work of Commission I-B was graciously undertaken by the already organized Pacific Coast Theological Group to which were added a few guests for the purpose at hand.

The volumes thus represent a combination of group thinking and individual effort. They are not designed to be completely representative statements to which the Commissions, or the Interseminary Movement, would subscribe. They are intended, rather, to convey information and to stimulate thought, in the earnest hope that this may in turn contribute to a more faithful performance of our Christian mission in the world.

For the National Interseminary Committee

ROBERT S. BILHEIMER

Executive Secretary

THE AUTHORS

John C. Bennett, whose A.B. is from Williams College, holds the B.A. from Oxford, the B.D. and S.T.M. from Union Theological Seminary in New York, and the D.D. from Church Divinity School of the Pacific and the Pacific School of Religion. He is professor of Christian theology and ethics in Union Theological Seminary. Among his publications are *Social Salvation*, *Christianity and Our World* and *Christian Realism*. Dr. Bennett is a member of the Congregational-Christian Church.

Elmer G. Homrighausen holds the A.B. degree from Mission House College, and the Th.B. degree from Princeton Theological Seminary. He has done graduate work at Chicago, Dubuque, Butler, Iowa and Rutgers universities and holds the Th.M., M.A., Th.D., and D.D. degrees. Dr. Homrighausen is professor of Christian education at Princeton Theological Seminary. Among his publications are *Christianity in America—A Crisis*, *Let the Church Be the Church*, *Choose Ye This Day* and *Evangelism*. Dr. Homrighausen is a member of the Presbyterian Church in the United States of America.

John Knox has his A.B. from Randolph Macon, his B.D. from Emory University and his Ph.D. from the University of Chicago. He is professor of sacred literature at Union Theological Seminary, New York. Among his publications are

The Man Christ Jesus, *Christ the Lord* and *Religion in the Present Crisis*, of which he is the editor. Dr. Knox is a member of the Methodist Church.

KENNETH SCOTT LATOURETTE holds the B.S. and D.D. degrees from Linfield College, and his B.A., M.A. and Ph.D. from Yale University, D.D. from MacMaster University, LL.D. from Denison University and Litt.D. from Baylor University. He is the D. Willis James Professor of Missions and Oriental History in Yale University. Among his publications are *The Chinese, Their History and Culture*, *Missions Tomorrow*, "A History of the Expansion of Christianity" series (7 vols.), *Anno Domini* and *The Unquenchable Light*. Dr. Latourette is a member of the Northern Baptist Convention.

RICHARD NIEBUHR has studied at Elmhurst College and Eden Theological Seminary, holds the A.M. degree from Washington University, and has the B.D. and Ph.D. degrees from Yale University. He is professor of Christian ethics in Yale Divinity School. His publications include *The Social Sources of Denominationalism*, *The Kingdom of God in America* and *The Meaning of Revelation*. Dr. Niebuhr is a member of the Evangelical and Reformed Church.

W. NORMAN PITTENGER holds the B.A. degree from Princeton and the S.T.M. from General Theological Seminary. He has studied also at Union Theological Seminary, Columbia and Oxford. Mr. Pittenger is instructor in Christian apologetics in General Theological Seminary and lecturer in religion in Columbia University. His most recent publications include *Worship*, *As His Follower*, *Christian Way in the Modern World*, *Stewards of the Mysteries of Christ*, *His Body the Church*, *The*

Divine Action, A Living Faith for Living Man. Mr. Pittenger is a member of the Protestant Episcopal Church.

PAUL SCHERER, whose B.A., M.A. and LL.D. are from the College of Charleston, also holds the B.D. from the Lutheran Theological Seminary, Philadelphia, the Litt.D. from Wittenberg College, and the D.D. from Roanoke College. After a distinguished parish ministry in New York, he recently became professor of practical theology in Union Theological Seminary there. His publications include *When God Hides, Facts That Undergird Life, The Place Where Thou Standest, For We Have This Treasure* and *Event in Eternity*. Dr. Scherer is a member of the United Lutheran Church.

LUMAN J. SHAFER holds the B.A., M.A. and Litt.D. from Rutgers University. He is the secretary of the Board of Foreign Missions of the Reformed Church in America. His publications include *The Christian Alternative to World Chaos* and *The Christian Mission in Our Day*. Dr. Shafer is a member of the Reformed Church in America.

INTRODUCTION

The Situation to Which the Volume Is Addressed

Kenneth Scott Latourette

Stocktaking is important in the life of the Church. From time to time Christians must seek to reappraise the Christian movement. They must be open-eyed to the perils which beset the Church and the faith of which it is the expression and the guardian. They must not seek to hide from themselves the weaknesses in the Church, even when, as is usually the case, these are there because they are their own imperfections and sins. Yet they must not permit their awareness of the enemies about them and within them to unnerve them. They must not take counsel of their fears. They must also keep in mind the achievements and the resources of the Church. They must hold ever before them the Christian confidence that the battle is ultimately not theirs but God's and that finally God must triumph.

Ours is a time when such stocktaking is peculiarly urgent. The human race is facing the most crucial era in its long history. All mankind is in revolution. Everywhere cultures are disintegrating and in flux. Through his intelligence man has developed processes and machines which are destroying the patterns of life and the institutions with which he has been familiar and which have shaped him. In the past three decades man has come through wars which have wrought destruction on an unprecedented scale. The geographic scope of the devastation arises from the fact that through his machines man has made his world a small neighborhood. Rapidly the globe has become "one world," as a startled statesman of our day discovered and proclaimed. Mechanical creations now in their infancy, such as the atomic bomb and planes with suprasonic speeds and directed by new electrical devices, carry the threat of wars which may obliterate the major cities of the globe and disrupt life to a degree which staggers and appalls the imagination. In his rough road man has known revolutions which have brought individual cultures to an end and many wars which have laid in utter waste larger or smaller segments of the globe. Never before, however, has the entire race been so on the march or so threatened by a vast cataclysm of its own making.

Has the Church the spiritual and moral resources to meet the crisis? It is clear that mankind's peril is primarily spiritual and moral. "We know the paths wherein our feet should press." We possess sufficient intelligence to devise programs for society and for an international order which would, if implemented, rescue mankind from its threatened doom and enable it to attain physical comfort and cultural advance far beyond its present dreams. What is lacking are the moral qualities essential to that implementation. These, in the last analysis, are in the realm of the spirit. Can man display the faith, the courage, the persistence, the regard for his fellows the world over, and the resolution to see that all individuals and groups around the globe have equal access to the good things of life, to enable him to rise above his petty personal, racial and national horizons and to work for the welfare of the whole until that welfare is attained? Here, as we are told until we are weary of hearing it, by statesmen, publicists, preachers, educators and scientists, lies the crux of humanity's problem. Can we look to the Church to fill this need? So many of us have said and believed. But must we not make a fresh appraisal of the Church and of the faith of which it is the expression and the custodian? Are the claims made for it justified? Do the Christian faith and the Church by their essential nature warrant us in looking toward them with such confidence? Have we a right to proclaim them to a pathetically, almost frantically eager world as the way to its health? Does the record of the Church and of Christianity justify such expectations? These are questions which will not down and which we must face and face now.

We must not prejudge the answers. We must not be content with facile and ready-made replies. Most of those who read the chapters which follow are committed to the Christian faith and the Church. Because of that commitment they come to the questions with a decided bias. Yet the very nature of our faith demands honesty. Christians must face with all the objectivity which they can command the questions which the age propounds to them. If the issue of their quest proves upsetting to their most cherished convictions they must not seek to evade it.

The following pages are designed to help us in that examination. They will have failed of their purpose if they are regarded as having given final formulation to the questions and their answers. They are meant to stimulate thought and to suggest materials which will assist those who come to them in the processes in which the authors as well as the readers are engaged. We and all thoughtful souls within the Church must face the problems here posed with all the frankness and the intelligence which we can command. Group discussion, the painful application of individual thought and meditation, and concurrent and subsequent action must all be employed if we are to arrive at the answers which are so urgently demanded by the world in which we live.

A glance at the table of contents will reveal something of the manner in which the authors of this volume have viewed their assignment. This particular book does not stand alone. It is one of a series. Only certain aspects of the problem are here considered. Additional phases are dealt with in the other volumes. Together all are meant to constitute a coherent whole.

As the title indicates, the present volume deals with the relation of the Christian gospel and the Church to the world. It is in three parts. The first has to do with the nature of the Gospel and of the Church. If we are to know what we are to expect of Christianity and the Church in the world of our day we must ascertain their genius. It would only be confusing to ask them to operate for ends and in ways which are not in accord with their basic and distinctive character. Obviously this demands that we first understand Jesus Christ and the revelation of God in Him. Here is the center of the Gospel. In the Incarnation is seen the fashion in which, according to the Gospel, God deals with man. We must next look at the Church and attempt to view it both as it is ideally and as it has expressed itself institutionally. We must inquire into its functions, the various conceptions of it held by different branches, and its unique and main features. We must seek to discover, too, what the Christian faith has to say of the nature of man and of history. We must ask whether we are in accord with the Gospel if we demand that it bring all of human society into conformity with its ideals. Are we requiring Christianity to do something which it regards as not in accord with its purpose when we seek from it deliverance of mankind and civilization from their present perils? The second portion of the volume endeavors to ascertain how the Gospel and the Church actually operate. There we begin with a survey which seeks to show the part which the Gospel and the Church have thus far played in human history and the direction in which they now seem to be moving. We then go on to the relation of the Church to society, inquire how the Church and the individual Christian should be expected to act, and raise the question as to whether we can anticipate the achievement of a society which fully conforms to the Christian gospel. We next face the inherent weaknesses and handicaps in which the Church is involved as it goes about its mission. In the third and final portion of the volume we endeavor to outline the task which the Church faces today. We inquire what reorientation is necessary in the thought and life of the Church if it is to fulfill its proper functions. We ask what individual Christians should do, what should be their qualities and what resources are available to them as they endeavor to accomplish their vocation.

There are the questions with which the writers have wrestled as they have striven, through these pages, to respond for themselves and for others to the urgent challenge of our times. They emerge from their labors with faith confirmed and augmented.

PART I. The Gospel

CHAPTER I

The Revelation of God in Christ

JOHN KNOX

CHAPTER II

The Nature of the Church

PAUL SCHERER

CHAPTER III

The Christian Hope of a Transfigured World

W. NORMAN PITTENGER

1

THE REVELATION OF GOD IN CHRIST

John Knox

1. The world by wisdom knew not God: The meaning of "the foolishness of God" and "the wisdom of man." The life everlasting. The kingdom of God. Faith in God. 2. We preach Christ: The "Lord Jesus Christ" as an event or closely related series of events, with the man Christ Jesus as its center. 3. God in Christ: an act of God, not a metaphysical concept. 4. Reconciling the world unto Himself: Christ and the new community: the total act of God as the ground of hope and faith. The ultimate wisdom of God. The story.

---

1. THE WORLD BY WISDOM KNEW NOT GOD

Several years ago I was a member of a group of men and women of the press who had been called together by a prominent churchman to listen to a discussion of plans for a great ecclesiastical gathering in a Midwest city. The principal matter yet to be decided (and the advice of the newsmen was sought on it) was who should be invited to make the "big speech" of the conference. We were told that four thousand delegates from every part of the nation would be present, that the resources of the city's largest hotels would be taxed to accommodate the crowds, that any number of well-known people would be present. Many of the speakers had been chosen. But who would the great speaker be? There was perhaps an hour's discussion of the question. The name of the man finally settled on is not important; it was the name of a politician then much in the news. But what did strike me as significant was the fact, which became more and more apparent as the discussion progressed, that the important criterion of the fitness of any proposed speaker was favorable social prominence. He must be a conspicuously successful politician, writer, banker, artist, industrialist. So far as I can remember, the question whether he had anything significant to say to this group of four thousand churchmen was not seriously raised. He must be a well-known man holding some important position and who would be willing to say some nice things about religion and the Church. Nineteen centuries ago the Pauls and Peters were compelling the Agrippas, the Felixes, and the Neros to listen to them, and often were paying for their boldness with their lives. I found myself wondering whether we had reached the point where the Church, without a distinctive and urgent message of her own, must bolster her sense of the importance of her mission by persuading the Agrippas, the Felixes and the Neros to say pleasant things about her and to her. I do not think so; I do not regard the incident I have related as typical; but it points up a danger in which the Church constantly stands: the danger of setting more store than she should by the good opinion of the great ones of this world, the peril of forgetting that with God there is no respect of persons, the temptation of violating her own integrity, of surrendering her own freedom, of failing to remember that "the weakness of God is stronger than men."

It is about the other side of Paul's paradox, however, that we are particularly concerned in this essay—"the foolishness of God is wiser than men"—and it is to another and subtler form of what is in reality the same danger that attention will be called. This is the danger, which confronts the Church in every age and has certainly done so in our own, of trying to enhance the prestige of its faith by bringing it completely under the aegis of a secular intellectualism. Speaking generally, we may say that Christianity, especially in its most creative epochs, has always maintained a vigorous intellectual life; it has nurtured and honored, and in turn been enriched by science and philosophy. Such a relationship is indispensable; without it we fall into a sterile and irrelevant fundamentalism or into a futile and dishonest obscurantism. But except in periods of decadence the Church has never brought itself to acknowledge the absolute supremacy of secular wisdom in the field of truth. It has insisted that in certain crucially important areas what may well seem foolishness to even the wisest of the children of this world is in reality the very wisdom of God.

This was certainly true in the primitive church. Christianity began magnificently. It stepped from the soil of Palestine on its westward march with the tread of a conqueror. It did obeisance to no man. It feared neither the wrath of men nor the wisdom of men. It worshiped neither the emperor nor the scholar. It did not sit at philosophy's feet; philosophy was soon sitting at its feet. For all its humble origin among Galilean peasants and workingmen—poor and unschooled—it became the teacher of Greece as it became the ruler of Rome. It did not for one moment acknowledge that truth to be true must pass the tests of the schoolmen. "God who spoke of old times through the mouths of His prophets has in these later days spoken through His son," declared these early preachers. In the assurance they felt of that fact and of all its implications they stood with head high and spoke with clear firm voice whether on a Philippian riverside or on the Athenian Areopagus.

But in recent years we have grown accustomed to taking for granted that man is the measure of all things; that the "word of God" is only a rather poetic way of referring to the voice of man's reason or conscience. We have found ourselves looking both wistfully and fearfully toward the laboratories of the scientists—wistfully, because we hoped they would conclude that Christian faith might be true after all; fearfully, because we expected on the whole that they would not. But that was not the attitude of the first Christian generation; they knew that their message was, according to the canons of what passed as good sense and strict logic, foolishness; they frankly called it such and then went out to prove that this foolishness was the foolishness of God and was wiser than men's wisdom.

The meaning of "foolishness" and "wisdom"

There are obviously two points being made here, and each of them calls for some elaboration. The first is that the Gospel is "foolishness" and the second is that it is the "wisdom of God." What does Paul mean by these two statements? Although he would not have formulated it in this way, I believe he meant something like this: When he says that Christian faith is foolishness, he means that it includes a much richer and fuller body of belief than can be justified by human wisdom, and that we cannot escape the option of either affirming the inadequacy of this wisdom or else of surrendering precious, indispensable and, to the Christian, self-evidently true elements of faith. There are some few but decisively important items of vital belief about which *this* can be said: every effort to *prove* them, that is, every attempt to establish their truth on universal and unquestionable grounds of reason and experience has both of two effects: first, it fails (one finds one cannot prove them), and, secondly, the attempt weakens the force of the beliefs themselves. A religious faith which can be proved does not deserve to be believed—ceases indeed to be a religious faith at all—and the more simple and plausible and easy we make Christianity, both on its ethical and its intellectual sides, the more commonplace and negligible we make it. This, or something like this, is what Paul means when he affirms that the Christian faith is foolishness.

But, says Paul, this foolishness is not the foolishness of ignorance or of intellectual irresponsibility or laziness; indeed, it is not foolishness at all. It is the wisdom of God. And here he means something like this: Wisdom, without the so-called folly of faith, fails even to be wisdom. The task of wisdom is to give an adequate and rational account of the world and the meaning of human life. It is likely to begin by seeing that faith is not *rational* and that therefore it must be excluded from such an account; but it will end by discovering that reason is not *adequate.* Wisdom thus finds itself rejecting what wisdom itself cannot dispense with. The lower wisdom aims at logic and sacrifices adequacy; the true wisdom aims at adequacy, and discovers a deeper logic. The world by wisdom only cannot be truly wise. The world by wisdom knew not God; and yet without the knowledge of God there can be no wisdom.

Three instances

By way of illustration of both of these points, consider three of the primary items in the Church's historic faith—primary not only in the sense that they have always belonged to it but also in the sense that the faith can hardly be conceived without them. Take, first, the belief in the life everlasting—the belief that life may be redeemed and fulfilled beyond the tragedy of death. One does not need to insist on the importance of this belief in the history of the Church. In a very real sense early Christianity sprang straight out of faith in the resurrection of Jesus. Without faith in the reality of that event the Church could never have come into existence, and without faith in the universal significance of this victory over death, the Church would have quickly perished. One could not begin to quote the hundreds of sentences in the New Testament in which this faith is expressed. The New Testament would be an altogether different book and Christianity would be an altogether different religion if we could not read: "Death is swallowed up in victory"; "What can separate us from the love of Christ? . . . Neither death nor life"; "An inheritance incorruptible . . . that fadeth not away"; and scores of similar phrases. This belief that human life is not doomed to end in futility and defeat (and is not that, when all is said, the alternative?)—this belief was not a mere wistful, half-romantic hope; it was a joyous, confident faith. . . . And yet who can prove it? Who indeed can render it plausible? Who that has looked upon the face of death can find sufficient rational grounds for even doubting, much less denying, its utter finality? Have you seen a loved one in the grip of some slow and fatal disease, like cancer or tuberculosis, watched the life ebb slowly from day to day, from month to month, perhaps from year to year, mind at each stage sharing the weakness of body, as each gradually disintegrates before one's eyes, until consciousness itself finally fails, and in the long coma which ensues death approaches so slowly that no one knows the moment of its coming? And could you look upon the wasted, twisted body that was left and still believe that death had not conquered? Such a belief when one confronts the stark reality of death is, in the light of ordinary reason, incredibly absurd and fantastic. And none of the facile apologias for the belief, which we are so fond of making, succeeds in doing more than to remind the reflective reader or hearer of its rational implausibility. And yet what sense does the world make, what meaning can be found in human life and history without it? Our lives are brief and transient, and we live on a planet which is soon to be destroyed. Will everything then be as though nothing had been? Our whole being—mind as well as heart—cries out against such a conclusion.

Or consider the Christian belief in the kingdom of God—the faith that there shall be a universal order of justice and peace, in which all the conflicts and frustrations of history will be overcome. That expectation is an intrinsic part of the Christian faith and has been from the beginning. But in the primitive church no one was under the illusion that it was a natural or sensible expectation. The early Christians could have given no philosophical or scientific grounds for it; it did not occur to them to try. In fact, they believed something so utterly grotesque that any attempt at that kind of justification is inconceivable. They believed that God would suddenly interrupt the processes of this natural world, destroy in a dreadful cataclysm all evil, root and branch, and in a moment of time establish His reign of righteousness among men. Imagine trying to make plausible so stupendous a faith! No one thought of trying. But we felt we must try, and so we began to justify our belief in the kingdom of God by specious appeals to biology and history. We convinced ourselves that all creation had been gradually moving, by easy and inevitable steps, toward the kingdom of God, and some of us were almost persuaded that we should not taste of death until we saw it. But the wise men of this world were not deceived, and now, as events force us to face the real character of the world we live in and as we read history in the light of that realization, we recognize that the faith that the kingdom is coming naturally is really as grotesque as that it will come miraculously, if not more so; that there is no way of making plausible from the human point of view the coming of the kingdom of God. And yet can it be true wisdom which reduces all of human life and history to "a tale that is told"?

Consider even the Christian faith in God: the belief that the maker of the heaven and the earth is good; that His righteous will is the law of life; that the hairs of our heads are numbered and that not a sparrow falls without His knowledge; that at the heart of this vast and complex universe, apparently so impersonal, if not mechanical, in its operations, there is eternal beauty and love, sufficiently personal and near for us appropriately to say, "Our Father." Was ever a belief from the point of view of ordinary wisdom more audacious, more fantastic? It has always been such, and, if possible, it is more than ever so today, somewhat because of the world view science has given us but more because the brutal character of large areas of man's life stands in these days so nakedly revealed. What can we do with all the evidences of a morally indifferent universe which lie about us on all sides? Is it plausible to believe God is love when whole nations starve? Or to believe He is even just when injustice lays daily its bitter burden upon the tired backs of millions of our fellow men? No, there is no adequate rational justification of the Christian faith that God, the maker of the heaven and earth, is a Father Almighty.

Wisdom or illusion?

What are we to say, then? Is our Christian faith built upon illusion? Is it foolishness—and not to the Greeks only? We utterly misunderstand Paul if we suppose that he is making any such admission. On the contrary he is making a proud boast. He is not confessing the limitations of his faith; he is asserting the limitations of human wisdom—the inability, that is, of reason to give an adequate account of the Reality with which men deal and on which they depend. He is affirming his own refusal to permit his faith in the significance of life to be confined within the neat, meager, abstract categories of the schoolmen. The "world by wisdom knew not God," but that was not an admission that God was not to be known, but rather that our human wisdom had not the last or truest word.

What was this last and truest word, this word of God? What was this divine wisdom, beyond discovery through man's effort, which provides the clew to the meaning of our existence? The strange answer was that the word was not a word at all, but an event—Christ crucified. The wisdom was not a wise saying but an illuminating deed. God had acted to make Himself known in an event of which the first Christians were witnesses. This event was the Lord Jesus Christ, whom their eyes had seen and their hands had handled. They knew that "God is and that He is the rewarder of those who diligently seek Him," not because they had thought through to that conclusion, but because God had revealed Himself in Christ. In this event—the living, dying and risen Christ—God had shined in their hearts and had lightened the darkness around them. They did not preach a new philosophy, but Christ crucified, which to those who did not really witness the event and thus became a part of it was a stumbling block and foolishness, but which to those to whom it was given to see it, was the power and the wisdom of God.

In a word, what the Church has been given to impart is not a philosophy, but a gospel, a "good news." The Christian message is not an argument, but an announcement—an announcement of an event which sets the whole meaning of human life in a new light. That event has happened, is happening, will happen (in the sense of being fulfilled); it has past, present and future reality and significance. The two succeeding chapters in this book will deal respectively with the event as it is happening still and as it is yet to be consummated; in this chapter we are thinking particularly about the event which *has* happened. We shall ask three questions about it: (1) What *was* the event? (2) What was the significance, or inner meaning, of the event? (3) What was the effect of the event? The answers to all of these questions have been already implied. Now they need to be more fully stated.[1]

2. WE PREACH CHRIST

The answer to the first of these questions has been more than once indicated: the event was the Lord Jesus Christ. This way of speaking may at first seem strange: to speak of a person as an event! It might be argued, of course, that in a certain very true sense such is what every person (and everything) is; but that is not quite our point. We mean, rather, that the phrase "the Lord Jesus Christ" does not designate simply a person; it designates a historical moment, the moment which the more primitive parts of the New Testament have "caught" for us and convey to us. Perhaps our meaning would be clearer if we spoke, not of an "event," but of a closely related series or cluster of events. The center of it is the person and career of Jesus, but included in it are such elements as the response of his disciples to him, the resurrection, the faith in the Son of God, the coming of the Spirit, the creation of the Church, the

[1] At best, these answers can be no more than suggested in this short essay. I hope to present them more adequately in a later book.

established Lordship of the living Christ. Indeed, it is, strictly speaking impossible to limit the event even to these factors. In a very true sense, the whole previous history of the Hebrew-Jewish community was a part of the event, as indeed are also the continuing Church and the final fulfillment. But within this larger context, it is surely possible and valid to identify a briefer moment of central and crucial significance. That moment, with all the essential elements belonging to it, is in our minds when we speak of "the Lord Jesus Christ."

This insistence upon an event—and an event in its rich, complex totality—as the medium of revelation is not a mere playing with words. A point of great importance for the understanding of the essential Christian message is involved. Indeed, it may be said that we have most frequently gone astray through attempts to define the medium of revelation more narrowly. The illuminating, saving event was one and indissoluble, and no effort to locate its whole significance in some fragment or aspect of it can succeed. It may be useful to consider briefly a few of the forms which such an effort can take.

A total event

Not infrequently the attempt has been made to divide between the "real" person, Jesus, and the response to him on the part of those who were intimately associated with him. The "real" event, it is held, must be "objectively" defined—that is, must be recognized as having occurred entirely outside the minds and hearts of those who witnessed it. To discover that event one must try to look *beyond* these witnesses, who although they alone could have led us *near* the event, now succeed only in hiding it from us. They show us what it meant to them and thus keep us from seeing what it was. Now if the word "Christ" designates simply and only a historical individual, something can perhaps be said for this view—although not too much, since it might be difficult to show that even such an individual can be thought of as having any reality apart from the responses which others make to him; certainly he could have no historical importance. But, however that may be, if "Christ" designates, not simply a person, but an event, then it is clear that the division between the objective and the subjective is impossible. One may try to *distinguish* the two elements—although one can never be altogether successful—and one may, and should, admit the subjective only with the greatest caution; but one cannot eliminate it entirely and still have a historical event. The primitive response to Jesus—what Jesus meant to those who knew him, how they received and remembered him—was as much a part of the total event as was Jesus himself. And the revelation was in and through that total event.

But equally fallacious is the attempt to divide as between the earthly life of Jesus and the resurrection, or between the "Jesus of history" and the "Christ of faith," and to find the revealing and saving efficacy only in the one or the other. From the moment of the Church's birth—and the revealing event cannot be said to have occurred till then—memory and faith were fused inseparably. Jesus was remembered by those who believed on him; he was believed on by those who remembered him. The memory was not a mere backward projection of the faith, as the "Christ-myth" people used to say; and the faith was not a mere forward projection of the memory, as many sounder historians have assumed. Each was firmly grounded in the experience of the primitive community. But the memory would not have been just what it was except for the faith, and the faith could not have been what it was without the memory. The one remembered was known still; the one known still was remembered. Gospels and epistles bring us the whole indissoluble event, and we cannot tear the two elements apart without destroying the New Testament.

If what has been said so far is true, one hardly needs to make the further point that any attempt to locate the point of revelation in some particular incident of Jesus' life or in some particular aspect of his nature is likewise misguided and futile. One cannot identify the event with the birth of Jesus, for example, and, in consequence, make its whole significance and effectiveness dependent in theory upon some particular understanding of the circumstances of Jesus' human origin. This will probably appear obvious enough to most of the readers of this essay, but there are other equally fallacious but more plausible simplifications. We cannot identify the revealing event with the consummate excellence of Jesus' moral character or with any (or all) of the gospel incidents in which this character is expressed. Nor can we find the whole event in the beauty, truth and strength of his religious and ethical teachings. It is likewise false to locate the event in the metaphysical nature of Jesus so that the recognition of his meaning is made to depend upon the acceptance of some particular definition of his person or his relation to God.

In the same way we must avoid locating the event solely in the death of Jesus. One says this with hesitation not only because of the importance which the death of Christ has always had in Christian theology, but also because it is the most holy place of Christian devotion. Indeed, it became supremely important in theology because it was first supremely important in devotion. Death is always likely to seem the most significant moment in the life of another; the death of Jesus was certainly the most significant moment in his life for those who had been his disciples and became the first Christian church. His whole meaning for them seemed to come to a focus there; it was inevitable that their attempts to explain this meaning should be drawn around that same center. But we must recognize that the death of Christ, as it is understood in the New Testament, is really symbolic of a more inclusive event. The meaning of that total event was most movingly manifest in the crucifixion, but the event was more than the crucifixion. The significance of the event does not derive from the death; on the contrary, the death has its great significance because it is a part—may we not say that it forms, with the resurrection, the very center? —of the whole event.

That event, I repeat, was one and indissoluble. The man Jesus, his teaching and his life, his death, his resurrection, the creation of the Church by the Spirit—these all participate in, and gather their meaning from, the one total event or cluster of events. When we speak of "the Lord Jesus Christ," we are thinking of this total historical reality. It is a personal reality because Jesus—living, dying and alive forevermore—is at the heart of it and pervades it in every part; but it is more than a person in any ordinary and simple sense. It is a person and all that happened in connection with him. It is nothing less than the supreme moment of human history.

3. GOD IN CHRIST

We come thus to our second question: What is the significance of the event? The answer here also has been anticipated: the event was an act of God. The thing that happened was something God *did*. This was not mere belief in the primitive church; it was faith. I mean by this distinction that this understanding of the meaning of the character, life, death, resurrection of Jesus, the coming of the Spirit and the creation of the community, in a word, the whole event we are discussing—this understanding was not a mere inference from the event or the result of reflection upon it; it was present in the event itself. Where there was no such faith, the event had manifestly not occurred; where the event had occurred, this faith was a part of it.

The faith grew, no doubt, with the event. As the event progressed the sense of God's action being in it became more and more lively, deep and sure. This awareness of God's action entered, in turn, as a creative element into the further shaping of the event. Thus, to repeat, this faith in the significance of the event as a deed of God is not the result of the event or something outside of it which later developed as men reflected upon it; it is of the warp and woof of the event itself. To be sure, there were those who, though acquainted in some sense with the man Jesus, were aware of no act of God in or through him; but these did not know the reality we have called "the Lord Jesus Christ." Indeed, the major difference between what the terms "Jesus" and "the Lord Jesus Christ" may be taken to designate lies just there. The members of the first Christian community were those whose eyes had been at least partly opened to the fact of God's action in Jesus and who, because of this awareness, could severally and together become factors in the further development of that event which in its wholeness (not excluding the awareness itself) is known in the New Testament and in Christian devotion as "the Lord Jesus Christ." This whole event *in its wholeness* was an act of God.

The act of God and the nature of Jesus

We go astray when we neglect either the word "act" in this sentence or the phrase "in its wholeness." Neglect of the word "act" betrays us into too great a preoccupation with the question of the *nature* of Jesus, which though important, is not the most important question. The most important question is not "Who (or what) *was* Jesus?" but "What was taking place in and through him? What did God *do* through him? What do 'the things which have happened among us' mean?" Paul's statement, which perhaps better than any single clause in the New Testament sums up not only his own gospel but also the gospel of the early church, "God was in Christ reconciling the world unto Himself"—this statement is an answer to this second question (variously stated), not to the first. The emphasis should be placed on the words "God," "Christ" and "reconciling"; not on the word "was." Paul is not making (in the manner of John's Prologue) a statement about the metaphysical nature of Jesus as though he would say simply, "God *was* in Christ." Rather, he is making a statement about the significance of an event: "What," he asks, "is the meaning of this wonderful thing that has happened (Jesus remembered and now risen, present Lord of a new community)?" He answers the question: "I will tell you: in Christ (i.e., in this great event) God was reconciling the world to himself."

The first Christology, even earlier than Paul, was almost certainly that represented by Acts 2:36: "God hath made that same Jesus, whom ye crucified, both Lord and Christ." But this is a statement, not about the metaphysical nature of Jesus, but about what God has done, is doing, and will do in and through him. Through him God will save His people—that is the central meaning of messiahship.

To be sure, once it was recognized that God had made such supreme use of Jesus and had exalted him to so supreme a status, it was inevitable that the question should be asked, "Who, then, *was* this Jesus, that he should have been the center of God's redeeming, reconciling action for all mankind?" But this, it should be made clear, was not the first question, either in time or in importance. And no answer given to it by the later church is as essential a part of Christian faith as was the first, spontaneous answer to the other question: "God has drawn near in Christ. He has visited and redeemed His people."

In such a statement there is no intention of discounting the importance of the great doctrines concerning the person of Christ worked out at Nicaea and Chalcedon. But that importance lies in the witness they bear to the reality and significance of God's *action* in history in and through the whole event we have been discussing rather than in their metaphysical accuracy. So taken, the ancient symbols can be a bond of unity and a safeguard of authentic Christian faith; taken otherwise, they become a stone for stumbling and an occasion of division within the Body of Christ.

It is appropriate to stress also that when we speak of the saving event as a mighty act of God, we are again thinking of the event as a whole. This does not mean that it was not also in every part a divine event. But each part was divine because it participated in a divine whole, not because it was divine in and of itself. The whole event was a miracle. To see this is to realize that it matters little whether any particular part of it was in some special or separate sense miraculous. The question of miracles in the New Testament becomes religiously and theologically important only when the miraculous character of the whole event is made dependent upon the answer we give to it. But the character of the whole event as an act of God cannot properly be made thus dependent. It made itself known as such quite apart from any particular miraculous incident or any number of such incidents together. The resurrection may appear to be an exception here; but the resurrection is more than a miraculous "incident." It is a mighty sign and symbol of the miraculous character of the whole event (Rom. 1:4). The resurrection was the moment when not only the spiritual Lordship of Jesus began ("Unless I go away, the Spirit cannot come"), but also when the whole earthly life was "transfigured before them," that is, seen in its true light —the moment when the event they had witnessed and were still witnessing was realized to be one whole and to be in its wholeness an act of God. Jesus, the center and symbol of that event, was thus the very Son of God.

4. RECONCILING THE WORLD UNTO HIMSELF

This brings us to our third question: What was the effect of this event? What has God done through Christ? Out of the experience of the primitive church comes a veritable flood of answers. He has revealed His love for us. He has forgiven us. He has saved us from our sin. He has given us joy that fades not away and peace that passes understanding. He has given us a lively hope of everlasting life. He has adopted us as His children and included us in "the kingdom of His dear Son." He has "shed abroad His love in our hearts through the Holy Spirit which has been given to us." He has reconciled us with Himself and with our brethren and has made us members of a new and wonderful fellowship. . . . And all of these benefits are not for us only, but for all men of every nation and kind. Jesus (again, the center and symbol of the whole event) is thus Saviour and Lord.

Do we dare go back of this spontaneous testimony of the early church and ask whether any of these answers takes precedence above the others, whether any of these effects can be thought of as more inclusive and decisive than the rest? I venture to suggest that we can. It will have been observed that in the various references which have been made to the elements belonging to the original revealing and saving event, the last element mentioned has always been "the creation of the community." In other words, *this* "effect" of the event is so immediate as properly to be regarded as a part of the event itself. We may say, then, that the first and most decisive consequence of Christ's coming is that through him God brought into existence a new people. We can see this beginning to happen long before the event reached its culmination at Pentecost. Jesus had drawn about him a company of disciples, who heard, loved and in some measure understood him; to them he had made himself known as living after his passion; and in this common memory and common experience it was realized that a new kind of community had come into being. This new community was the gift of God, not something they had made. It was nothing less than the Spirit of God in their midst. They had been caught up into a divine fellowship—a fellowship with the living Christ and with one another around him.

The Lord and the new community

With the meaning of this fellowship and with the fruits of it the next two chapters are to be concerned. Here we shall consider it, very briefly, first, as the medium or carrier of forgiveness and new life, and, secondly, as the ground of faith and hope.

First, then, it was in this community with Christ and with one another around him that reconciliation and new life were found. Christ, as we have seen, did not exist in a vacuum; nor was he known by individuals in their separateness. Individuals, apart from others, may have had some acquaintance with what we are pleased sometimes to call "the historical Jesus," but the reality we have been discussing in this chapter, "Jesus Christ the Lord," could only be corporately known. Individuals could, of course, be conscious of personal fellowship with Christ, but they had this fellowship as members of the group through which the love of God in Christ was mediated. So true is this that the very term "Christ" seems at times in the New Testament to be used to designate the community, his Body, as often in Paul's phrase "in Christ."

Now this knowledge of Christ was a knowledge of God wanting to reconcile and be reconciled, ready to forgive, moving us to penitence and trust, offering us both pardon and a new righteousness. Do not ask *why* this should have been true; why there should have been this connection between the event we have been considering and God's revealing and reconciling act. There have been many attempts to explain why only in Christ's presence could God make Himself known, in just the way He did, as holy and forgiving love. None of these attempts has been successful, although most of them serve to remind us of facets of a Reality which is as far beyond our power of explanation as God's thoughts are higher than our thoughts. But however inadequate and earth-bound, not to say age-bound, all the *explanations* of the atonement have been, there can be no doubt of the fact of it. These first believers had been hopelessly lost; now their feet were set in a firm, clear path. They had been strangers or enemies, divided within themselves and against others; now they were at home. They had been bound by fear and sin; now they were free—free not by any moral achievement of their own, but by God's mercy moving through the event they had witnessed and of which they had been made a part. The holy and loving God, making Himself known to them through Christ, had brought them to repentance and had reconciled them to Himself. That reconciliation, being restoration to their true nature and destiny, meant life and peace.

But this same experience of the Spirit within the life of the community meant also confidence and hope. It was the source and ground of the early church's faith in the meaning of life and of hope for its fulfillment. Paul tells us that three things abide—faith, hope and love—and that the greatest of these is love. Love *is* the greatest, because faith and hope are grounded in it. The abounding, triumphant faith and hope of the primitive community were based on no argument, as we saw at the beginning of this chapter; they sprang from the reality of the love of God in its own life. The love of God had been shed abroad in their hearts by the Holy Spirit, and it was this love, already present, which made them sure that their hope would not disappoint them. Their faith in the ultimate meaning of life and their hope of its ultimate fulfillment (and can either of these long exist without the other?) was more than a mere belief, however tenaciously held and boldly proclaimed and defended; it was a serene and indomitable confidence based upon what had already come to pass. The love already shed abroad in their hearts, the Spirit already given, permitted of no doubt or fear. God had already spoken His redeeming Word; would he take that Word back? God had already begun His saving work in Christ: was it credible, or even thinkable, that He would not complete it? This faith and hope were foolishness to the Greek; but to those who had witnessed God's saving act, the only possible wisdom.

The ancient story

This wisdom of God, thus based in an event, the first Christian generation embodied in a story—a great, a tragic, a triumphant story. If they had been speaking mere wisdom, they might have expressed it otherwise—as we have since then tried to do—in a metaphysic or a science. But what they had to say—and what we have to say, if we only knew it—was too great for any such terms to hold it. Only a story would do, and here was the story: One, who shared the nature and throne of God and resided in the heavenlies, out of love of mankind—of all mankind, of every race, nation and class—was willing to renounce His godliness, to take on the nature of a common man, to enter fully and without reservation into our human life, sharing its limitations, its frustrations, its loneliness and suffering, from birth to bitter death at the hands of blind and brutal men. But death was not able to hold Him. He rose from the dead. He was exalted to the heavenly estate which He had previously surrendered, only now He possessed it not by right of nature but by the surer right of suffering. . . . But why should we paraphrase when we can listen to Paul's very words: "Let this mind be in you," he writes to the Philippian church, "which was also in Christ Jesus, who being in the form of God, thought not equality with God a prize to be grasped, but emptied himself, took upon himself the form of a slave, and was made in the likeness of men; and being found in fashion as a man, he still further humbled himself, and became obedient unto death, even the death of the cross. Wherefore God also hath highly exalted him and given Him a name which is above every name, that at the name of Jesus every knee should bow, of things in heaven, and things on earth and things under the earth, and that every tongue should confess that Jesus Christ is Lord to the glory of God the Father."

It is not for a new metaphysic or a new science that our age dies—that its heart dries up. It is for a fresh telling and a fresh believing of that ancient story. Is not that what Will Durant is saying when he writes, "We move into an age of spiritual exhaustion and despondency like that which hungered for the birth of Christ"? Christ must be born again. The old story must be told again, told in such fashion that men again will hear it, again will understand its meaning, again will believe its truth—its truth not as a series of mere incidents in ancient history, but as a timeless representation of the inner meaning of that event in which alone the righteousness and the forgiving love of God and the ineffable meaning of human life were with some adequacy revealed. The story has not lost its ancient power; it cannot, so long as man is man and the world is the world. It is a mighty affirmation that God is our Creator, Judge, Redeemer, Companion; that man, made in His image, standing every moment under the judgment of His righteous will, is also the object of His love—a love which knows and in some strange way shares our human agony, a love which broods like a mother over the tragic scene of man's short days and in which all the suffering generations live and move and find their rest at last. Without such faith man cannot bear to live. To the sophists, and the sophisticates, it may continue to be foolishness, but to those who would live greatly, even in such a world as ours, it is and will always be the power of God and the wisdom of God.

Further Reading

BAILLIE, JOHN and MARTIN, HUGH. *Revelation.* New York: The Macmillan Company, 1937.

CRAIG, CLARENCE TUCKER. *The Beginning of Christianity.* New York: Abingdon-Cokesbury Press, 1943.

DODD, C. H. *The Apostolic Preaching.* Chicago: Willett, Clark & Company, 1937.

MANSON, W. *Jesus the Messiah.* Philadelphia: Westminster Press, 1946.

PITTENGER, W. NORMAN. *Christ and Christian Faith.* New York: Round Table Press, 1941.

2

THE NATURE OF THE CHURCH

Paul Scherer

1. The meaning of the question: a growing rediscovery, the basic issue. 2. The Church in its origin and history: the covenant established, the covenant renewed, a new community, the community and the world. 3. The Church as fact and idea: the churches and the Church, the emerging fellowship. 4. The Church as community: true self-realization, the reassertion of community. 5. The Church as vehicle and agent. 6. The Church as worshiping community: liturgy, thought and Sacraments. 7. The Church militant and triumphant: continuing struggle, ultimate victory.

1. THE MEANING OF THE QUESTION

A growing rediscovery

It would not be very difficult to document the fact, and do it elaborately, that the Protestant church, if one may use such a term, has not only begun to move, but has recently been moving with a kind of cumulative rapidity, toward a new awareness of itself and of its underlying catholicity. Never since the Reformation, never in fact since the early centuries of Christianity, has the sense of a common heritage in faith and fellowship struggled so insistently to the front. There are those, indeed, who find in this struggle, and not without good reason, one of the most significant patterns of our time.

Obviously, a measure of this progress toward self-awareness has come about by way of inevitable reaction to the immediate pressure of events, and by that token may measurably disappear when the pressure is relaxed. But surely not without some permanent deposit. It can hardly be for nothing that under direct and frontal attack in many lands, compelled to maintain at least the innermost lines of a consistent witness against the world, Protestantism has been driven as rarely before to a consciousness of its essentially ecumenical character.

Nor is that the whole story. Faced by the necessities of self-preservation, the great historic Protestant bodies have discovered each its separate weakness and together their common strength. Far from being unable to resist the onslaught of barbarism, they have found in their keeping, somewhat it would seem to their own surprise, what with increasing urgency commends itself to thoughtful minds as the only alternative to a depersonalized and dehumanized existence.

We live in a world divided, gone berserk with individualism: and afraid, deathly afraid. The centrifugal forces that have been at work throughout the modern era have so utterly disrupted human society as to have brought humanity itself to the verge of extinction: while man's notion of his own being, even as a child of nature, his conceptions of truth and liberty, of justice and mercy, have suffered under the acids of "scientism," of instrumentalism and positivism, such irreparable loss; his purchase in the universe has been rendered so unsecure, his aims so irrelevant, his destiny made to seem so obviously trivial, that nothing is left for him apparently but to hide his face in what Berdyaev has called some monstrous "collectivism that has no face!" Either that, or else—

No longer to worship each his own Messiah, in some illusory flight of the alone to the Alone. No longer in an ecstasy of freedom to fashion each his own religion, that ultimate insanity of the would-be untrammeled mind. No longer in the brief interludes of his solitary quest, each for his own pot of gold at the foot of his own rainbow, to chase each his own private butterfly of pious sentiment. But to enter again into his birthright as a child of God, in a sacramental fellowship which is itself God's own creation: where there is neither Greek nor Jew, Barbarian, Scythian, bond nor free; where all that still divides is seen in its true perspective against the background of all that can still unite; and where, by the realization of a self redeemed in a community of grace, he can rise as from no merely human context toward the fullness of his proper stature in Christ Jesus.

What then is the true nature of the Church? So little have we understood it that many of us find ourselves unable to define the word itself with any accuracy. In popular usage it may mean no more than an edifice, or the group that worships there. It may mean, reaching out, the denomination to which that group adheres, or the sum total of all such groups in the community or in the world. When the sociologist thinks of it, he tries to think of it objectively, in empirical terms. He applies to it norms that often enough have very little to do with religion and less to do with Christianity. He attempts to differentiate it from other corporate bodies on the basis of certain observable criteria which turn out to be altogether too arbitrary and not one of them decisive. Nor is the theologian in a very much happier case. On Monday, Tuesday and Wednesday he may well lose both himself and the object of his search in some Platonic realm of invisible ideas, having hardly any contact at all with reality, their *locus* somewhere in heaven above, nothing but their shadow on the earth beneath. On Thursday, Friday and Saturday he is likely to become involved in the complexities of an institution, with its panoply of priest and sacrament, which he forthwith makes the keeper of the keys, or absolutizes as the kingdom of God. Over here the Church is the Body of Christ. Over there it is an association of believers. In between it is the company of the called.[1] One wishes to recognize it by its ethics. Where there is race prejudice, it has been suggested, there is no Church. Where the Word of God is rightly preached, insisted the Reformers, and the sacraments are rightly administered, there is! Perhaps the best that ever can be done is to do as they did: to answer the question by begging it!

The basic issue

Because the question itself is almost never raised in any form that makes anything else possible. When we ask it we are usually engaged in deciding who "belongs," and who doesn't; who is really a Christian, and who isn't; with whom we may wholeheartedly co-operate, and from how many others we must keep ourselves separate. Leaving aside our consciousness of the family itself, we devote our efforts to the tracing out of the family tree. We are like people strolling in the zoo. We look at the lion and describe it; but there is no *lion-ness* (!) in the description. What we say, he would hardly understand. If he did, it might even annoy him! The problem with which the Church confronts us is like every other problem of being

[1] See *The Nature of the Church*, A report of the American Theological Committee, of the Continuation Committee of the World Conference on Faith and Order (Chicago: Willett, Clark & Company, 1945).

when you keep pushing at it. Nothing but an existential approach offers any promise of solution. Which is to say that in the case before us, and for our purposes, the question has to arise in the area of faith, of divine encounter and human response; and it must find its ultimate answer there if anywhere. Actually we are set here to affirm what it is that *from within* constitutes the Christian Church; beneath the differences that make us many, to uncover the reality that makes us one.

When the question is put in that form, the answer which springs immediately to our lips is that the Church is a unique fellowship of grace called into being by a divine act and resting on the foundation of God's revelation in Christ. We are able to speak of its uniqueness and its fellowship, of grace and act and revelation, because we are aware in ourselves of a calling and a deed, of a bond and a Presence and a redeeming power, which here as nowhere else came alive with meaning. From this household, as from some ancestral home, the whole world takes on for us a different aspect. Time unfolds in another kind of history. We play our part in the common life of men; but its joys and its sorrows, its success and its failure, its triumphs and catastrophes, are no longer the same. They are the endless mercies of God and His unsearchable judgments. They are the ways past finding out. We move among events, but we do not belong to them. They have lost their power ultimately to shape us. We are set as co-workers with that sovereignty which shapes them. There are always the traditions of another country, where God has made Himself known. There is the language of another people, its accent, its customs. The years have another frame of reference. We are a colony of heaven. We stand in the grace of our Lord Jesus Christ, the love of God, and the communion of the Holy Ghost.

2. THE CHURCH IN ITS ORIGIN AND HISTORY

That communion was mediated to us in time through a community divinely chosen. Whenever and wherever along the course of the centuries God has revealed Himself, there has always resulted some kind of fellowship; and always both the character of that fellowship and its function have been conditioned by, though never dependent upon, the degree and extent to which the revelation was apprehended and expressed.

The covenant established

It was this persistent and universal self-disclosure, by whatever other act and counsel of that inscrutable Will which broods over human history, which gave uniquely among the Jews form and substance to "the people of God." Of Abraham, called out of Ur of the Chaldees into a place which he should after receive for an inheritance, was shaped a family; out of a family a tribe, and out of tribes a nation: that the kingdom or rule of the Eternal might within the created order establish itself both as goal and culmination. Through rebellion and judgment, through repentance and deliverance, now captive, now free, moved the assembly of "the first-born," forever haltingly, over and again bogging down completely; until all the promise of the Old Testament, and all its tragedy, are seen to be bound up in the gradual falling away of these children of the covenant: as their members dwindle, no more than a poor sifted tenth is left, a scrap, a fragment; and now but One, when the fullness of time was come, who solitary in suffering and solitary in triumph sets Himself to be His people's destiny!

The covenant renewed

In Him was the covenant renewed, and the Israel of God reconstituted "a royal priesthood, a holy nation," "born not of blood, nor of the will of the flesh, nor of the will of man," yet heir to the promise. Between the first community, fashioned not by their own loyalties but by the creative Word and Act of Him Whom the prophets proclaimed as both the Judge of History and its Redeemer, between that "seed of Abraham" and the Christian Church, called into being by the life and death and resurrection of Jesus of Nazareth, there is direct, organic and uninterrupted continuity.

Certainly in the teaching of our Lord this company of those who would endure steadfast in his love, obedient to his commandment, was at least implicit. Without entering at all into the Messianic problem, the very number of the Twelve could hardly be other than symbolic of the new Israel. Here from the beginning was something more than an informal fellowship of believers. It was to their shared faith that the offer was made of resources beyond their own. On them was the charge laid to publish the good news of a kingdom that had already begun to make its presence felt with power. Into their keeping was committed that apostolic witness to the risen, regnant Christ which was itself the charter of the new dispensation. It was upon them, with one accord in one place, that there came a sound from heaven as of a rushing mighty wind, to fill all the house where they were sitting.

Theirs was no independent religious society, constituted by the supreme revelation of God in Christ. Rather did the revelation take place *within* the society. The Hebrew *Qabal*, that assembly convened by Yahweh to be a blessing in the midst of the land, set apart for His name, had become the Christian *ecclesia,* established as itself the ground of the revelation, without which no revelation would have been possible. From it has come down to us the record of those words and events by which it was called into being: words and events which are themselves the gospel of Jesus Christ, as he made himself known to men, "in the circle of his associates and their successors, before His death and after, living, dying and alive forevermore, God drawn wondrously near as grace and truth." [2]

From the very beginning on to the days of Jeremiah, through Joel to the Preaching of the Apostles, the line runs straight.

> This shall be the covenant that I will make with the house of Israel; after those days, saith the Lord, I will put my law in their inward parts, and write it in their hearts; and will be their God, and they shall be my people. And they shall teach no more every man his neighbour, and every man his brother, saying, know the Lord: for they shall all know me, from the least of them unto the greatest of them, saith the Lord: for I will forgive their iniquity, and I will remember their sin no more.
> Jer. 31:33-34.

> And it shall come to pass afterward, that I will pour out my spirit upon all flesh; and your sons and daughters shall see visions. Joel 2:28.

> For this cause I bow my knees unto the Father of our Lord Jesus Christ, of whom the whole family in heaven and earth is named, that he would grant you, according to the riches of his glory, to be strengthened with might by his Spirit in the inner man; that Christ may dwell in your hearts by faith; that ye, being rooted and grounded in love, may be able to comprehend with all saints what is the breadth, and length, and depth, and height; and to

[2] John Knox, *Christ the Lord* (Chicago: Willett, Clark & Company, 1945), p. 73.

> know the love of Christ, which passeth knowledge, that ye might be filled with all the fulness of God. Eph. 3:14-19.

So it was that on the day of Pentecost the "Covenant in His blood" was constituted a Fellowship of power in the Holy Ghost. Writes R. Newton Flew:

> The message which they *had* accepted and which the rest of Israel had rejected was that of God's final salvation; to accept *it* was to go into the Kingdom . . . to reject it was to stay outside. Their mission *now* was to deliver it . . . and in the delivery of it they were *henceforth* fully commissioned representatives of the Son of man. . . . To reject them was to reject God Himself.[3]

The followers of Jesus were hereafter to be denied his person; but by his mighty act they had been redeemed in and into the company of the redeemed, the very function of which was redemption. The saving work of the Messiah was accomplished. The Son was enthroned at the right hand of God the Father. On earth was no Jesus cult. On earth was a kingdom indwelt by Another Who testified of Him, bringing all things to their remembrance.

A new community

And to such effect that these few, these "happy few," this "band of brothers," not only fancied themselves to be God's fresh creation: they were! Of them, somewhere about the middle of the second century, the author of the Epistle to Diognetus says:

> [They] are distinguished from other men neither by country, nor language, nor the customs which they observe. . . . As citizens, they share in all things with others, and yet endure all things as if foreigners. . . .

[3] R. Newton Flew, *Jesus and His Church* (New York: Abingdon-Cokesburg Press, 1938), p. 122. Changes and omissions indicated.

> They obey the prescribed laws, and at the same time surpass the laws by their lives. They love all men, and are persecuted by all. . . . They are poor, yet make many rich. . . . When punished, they rejoice as if quickened into life. . . . Those who hate them are unable to assign any reason for their hatred. . . . [They] are confined in the world as in a prison, and yet they are the preservers of the world. . . . [They] dwell as sojourners in corruptible [bodies], looking for an incorruptible dwelling in the heavens. . . . God has assigned them this illustrious position, which it were unlawful for them to forsake.[4]

It was in such fashion that they set about the mission to which the old Israel had proved faithless: these people that "turned the world upside down," . . . saying not that the kingdom of God is outside history, but that in the midst of history "there is another king, one Jesus" (Acts 17:6,7). They were a few hundred men and women to begin with, of no standing, with no wealth. Through martyrdom they moved up out of obscurity. They set themselves with their Scriptures and their bishops and their rule of faith against a pagan culture. When three hundred years had passed the symbol of that faith had climbed upon the standards of the Empire, and the Church was suddenly faced with what is perhaps the profoundest question of its own existence: Just how shall the community of believers relate itself and its life to the national or world community within which it has to live?[5]

The community and the world

To that question throughout the centuries there have always been two answers: one of them inclusive, resulting through

[4] *The Ante-Nicene Fathers,* Roberts and Donaldson (New York: Charles Scribner's Sons, 1908), Vol. I, p. 26 f.

[5] John Baillie, *What Is Christian Civilization?* (New York: Charles Scribner's Sons, 1945), p. 6.

the Middle Ages in the emergence of the Holy Roman Empire, a more or less homogeneous framework within which the very principle of unity was a "derivative" from the unity of the Christian faith; the other always tending toward some form of sectarianism, forever "gravely disturbed at the admixture of worldly living" which had found its way into the Christian fellowship, from generation to generation "entering the same kind of protest against the apostasy of the wider Church as the Hebrew prophets had made against the national community of Israel."

This steadily if somewhat irregularly growing tension reaches its breaking-point in the Reformation. From within the body of an already disintegrating Christendom came the decisive revolt against that portion of it which, embracing the world to save the world, had lost sight of itself in the embrace, and of the end it had once intended to serve. There was at first no thought in the mind of the Reformers to destroy the visible one-ness of "the body of Christ." There was only the thought to convert, to turn again and restore. But factors were at work now in human history that could not be so simply controlled as in times gone by. In a weird ecstasy of what it thought was freedom, the West began to strike off the shackles not only of false doctrine but of all doctrine, setting out sturdily on the road to moral anarchy. The Church gradually lost her hold. Religion became a private affair. It was the way you felt about God. Theology grew more and more suspect. Sin no doubt was ignorance. Knowledge no doubt was power. To set off humanity's arrogance, there was stamped on its flesh the Seal of its Simian ancestry. In the dark caverns of its mind were the steady, padded footfalls of the beast. Man little by little learned to negate all value, to despise himself, to anathematize his own kith and kin with bell, book and candle, and once and for all to abandon the inner for the outer. The State at least was real. Blood and race and soil were real. The world was his oyster who had the sword to open it!

3. THE CHURCH AS FACT AND IDEA

How on earth then is it still possible under such circumstances to talk of the Church, and still to believe in it? Especially when you realize that what we actually see in front of our eyes is manifestly *not* a Church, but a miscellany of churches. There are 256 of them in America that are listed as Protestant. They are not only confusing: they are both inwardly and outwardly confused. They are more than imperfect: they are in themselves a *reductio ad absurdum* of the very idea inherent in the word fellowship; with their strange emphases, their varying practices and beliefs, their class distinctions, their national loyalties, their pride and exclusiveness, their rivalries and prejudices and antipathies. The many are patent enough. Where is the one?

The churches and the Church

It is, of course, no final solution of the problem simply to point out and point up the difference between the Church as God knows it and the churches which we encounter: to call the one invisible and take refuge in it; while accepting the other as visible, quite sure that nothing can be done about it. Augustine, from whom the formula of "visible" and "invisible" was borrowed during the early years of the Reformation, had no such notion of the relationship that exists between the two. To him that relationship was dynamic, not static. There was a Church above history, and a Holy Catholic Church within history; the latter not so much a being as a becoming. It was the invasion of Time by Eternity, the City of Man by the City of God. It was a continuous shaking clear of the Body of that Christ Who was neither "Lo, here," nor "Lo, there"; but "Lo, I am with you always!" There was a Realm on earth that was more than idea: it was fact. But it was not of necessity demonstrable fact, responsive to the senses. There were gifts of the Spirit; but they were not under compulsion today and tomorrow to be outwardly discerned. There was a "terrestrial kingdom where dwelt also the celestial," each with its "various citizens"; only in this world were they mingled.[6] There were "two cities: one whose end is eternal peace, called Jerusalem; the other whose joy is temporal peace, called Babylon. . . . And Jerusalem is held captive in Babylon, but not all; for the angels also are its citizens." There were "two kinds of men: the one trusting in earthly things with which this world abounds, the other confiding in heavenly things, which God, Who doth not lie, hath promised."[7]

With these relativities of human history the Reformers were considerably less impatient than we, being far more interested in the *source* of unity than in its conspicuousness. To this they adhered as passionately as they knew how, testifying to that adherence in their very refusal to acquiesce in the identification of a corporate, "realistic" and temporal institution with the no less corporate, no less "realistic," but eternal fellowship of believers. There was no organization that was the Commonwealth of God. Yet they declined to assume that what could not be seen was therefore certain to be fanciful and unreal.

[6] Erich Przywara, *An Augustine Synthesis* (New York: Sheed & Ward, Inc., 1936), p. 271.

[7] *Ibid.*, p. 270.

> We are speaking [they wrote] not of an imaginary Church, which is to be found nowhere; but we say and know certainly that this Church, wherein saints live, is and abides truly upon earth; namely, that some of God's children are here and there in all the world, in various kingdoms, islands, lands and cities, from the rising of the sun to its setting, who have truly learned to know Christ and His Gospel.[8]

The emerging fellowship

To speak of it continually as an ideal in prospect, some day to be realized, is therefore to empty words of their meaning. The situation is not unlike that of the whole human race. There *is* a one-ness of mankind which man will not apprehend; nor will he live in recognition of it. He cannot deny it; he can only betray it, and in the betrayal destroy himself. So here the Church of God is a fact already accomplished. There is a flock not scattered, but gathered; imperfect, yet being made perfect; within history now, as its consummation hereafter; coming up, as the lights and shadows of a portrait begin to form in the coating of a film under the acid, or as a figure that keeps materializing through the fog of all our human relationships, into a living image of what this torn world of ours could be in the healing grip of that strange man on a cross. We have to do with a society, as Richard Niebuhr has put it, which is at the very edge of coming into existence, not yet to be seen, but more real than all the communities which are passing away; an emergent, as mind was an emergent through the long ages, the most powerful thing in the world, though not yet conscious of itself, and in that sense invisible.[9] It is a fellowship moving persistently into the world of events, not to be denied, betrayed at our peril, restoring and being itself restored, never destroyed

[8] *The Apology to the Augsburg Confession,* ch. IV.

[9] Richard Niebuhr, *Religion in Life,* winter number, 1945-46, p. 114.

but always being fulfilled, existing not of itself but of the spirit of God. We should be rejecting the deepest knowledge we have of it if we should say anything less.

That from the very beginning it should assume, now in this place, now in that, its own diversified and outward forms, was inevitable. From within, by struggle and conflict, working and being wrought, building and built upon, it has fashioned the structure which is yet more than anything else an accident, not indeed the substance, of its being. Impose on it the limits of its own primitive simplicity, whether in thought or practice, as if those limits themselves had somehow been divinely ordained, and you cast aside the wealth and experience of twenty centuries. You deny great areas of its life in your effort to revive it. With the error to which it is subject, you discard the truth to which it is drawn. Nor is there any escape in the opposite direction by way of an order conceived of in other than functional terms, or a ministry which derives its authority from some source and sanction other than the Gospel itself which creates the Church. This would be to subvert the very spirit of the New Testament by the annulment of freedom; and to disallow the saving grace of God which by its own means through Word and Sacrament, and not by human appointment, calls as it will and gathers, enlightens where it can and sanctifies: "in which Christian Church" the workmanship itself of God's Holy Spirit, "He daily forgives abundantly all my sins, and the sins of all believers, and will raise up me and all the dead at the last day, and will grant everlasting life to me and to all who believe in Christ."[10]

The perennial nature of our dilemma then, as long as humanity remains human, lies in the fact that no sharp line of demarcation can be drawn between this one, holy, Catholic, apostolic Church and that other Church, other and not other,

[10] *Luther's Small Catechism, The Creed,* Article III.

which to our earthly senses is indeed not one and far indeed from being holy. Here are but the two aspects, divine and human, of the same reality; "latent" and overt; hidden and manifest; the kingdom that is not of this world, but in it; the foolish things, the weak things, the base things, the things despised, which God hath chosen, yea, the things which are not, to bring to nought the things that are, lest any flesh should glory in His presence. The boundary between the things that are and the things that are not, yet bring them to nought, is not an outward boundary between concrete phenomena: rather is it an inner boundary between two states of the human soul. The one may contend against the other in the very act of being fulfilled in it. There is tension, not separation. A belonging to history and a transcending of it. The Church as it is, and the Church as God is shaping it: that He might present it to Himself holy and without blemish, not having spot, or wrinkle, or any such thing: and the nations of them which are saved shall walk in the light of it. And the gates of that city shall not be shut.

In the words of Bishop Brent, it is

> a city of magnificent distances. Its might and myriad breath are the same—limitless; in it are great extremes, not contradictory, but complementary. He who lives at one extreme reaches his largest liberty when he can visit the opposite extreme without losing his way. If, however, he goes only with abuse on his lips and missiles in his hand, in God's name let him keep to his own corner of the city. It is not safe for himself or others to walk about. The beauty and proportion of the city are spoiled when you narrow its boundaries. It is of the essence of unfairness to read out of the city a fellow citizen because he lives in a distant street with which you are not acquainted.[11]

[11] Quoted by William Jewett Tucker, *The Function of the Church in Modern Society* (Boston: Houghton Mifflin Company, 1911), pp. 28-29.

Meanwhile those who love that city most are most aware of its failures. W. A. Visser 't Hooft has a little book which he calls *The Wretchedness and the Greatness of the Church.*[12] In the very title alone appears the continuing paradox of all things human. The wretchedness of the Church consists not in its weakness, but in its refusal of strength; not in its finitude, but in the pride that sets itself in the way of the Infinite; not in the relativities of its temporal lot, but in its substitution of them for the absolute and the Eternal. What it has to fear is not so much infiltration from the world, but rather love of the world. This is secularism. It is not in danger of being colored by the life around it; it *is* that life caught up into another dimension whenever it will turn its face Godward. And there lies its greatness: not in anything that it accomplishes, but in the fact that it is itself both the organ and the object of God's redemption; its uniqueness determined by the character of its Founder, its holiness by the creative brooding of His Spirit, its apostolic mission by His continuous appointment.

4. THE CHURCH AS COMMUNITY

To see it at all, therefore, we must see it as part of His eternal plan with the shadow resting on it:

> Listen, you who are deaf,
> And you who are blind, look and see.
> Who is blind but my servant?
> Or deaf like the messenger I send? Isa. 42:18-19

It was the shadow then as now of a people standing in the light of that purpose which would not suffer defeat.

> Behold, Jacob, my servant, whom I uphold;
> Israel, my chosen, in whom my soul delighteth.

[12] (London: Student Christian Movement Press, Ltd., 1944.)

I, the Eternal, have called thee,
I have grasped thee by the hand,
I have kept thee and made thee my pledge to the nations.
Isa. 42:1, 6

True self-realization

The stubborn pathos of all the ages is reflected in those lines. The situation in which human life perpetually finds itself may be represented as an ellipse described around two foci. On the one hand is a tremendous drive toward the realization of an independent self-hood, with all the rebellion against both God and man which that seems to entail: a spirit that deaf and blind to everything else ever and again asserts its explosive energies in a demonic will to separateness. On the other, a no less persistent and no less ineradicable urge toward community, of which God Himself is the energizing and undergirding fact: "Israel, my chosen, my pledge to the nations." It is when in any given historical period too few understand the identity of these two apparently divergent not to say opposite quests, that the pathos turns promptly into tragedy. No fulfillment of either is ever possible except as the other is fulfilled.

In this lay the ruin of Germany. What the Nazis saw was that "man finds himself by subordinating himself to the group." The Christian gospel sees that. "Ye are members one of another." But it was only half a truth. The Christian gospel preserves the other half as well. "It is the will of your Father which is in heaven that not one of these little ones should perish." What the Nazis forgot was that "the group attains its goal only by serving" the individual. "Personal freedom," writes Jacques Maritain, "is the love of social life"; and social life is "a complex of human freedoms which accept obedience

. . . in order to enable each of these freedoms to reach . . . a truly human fulfillment."[13]

One may justly contend that the people of Israel came nearer this achievement of self-hood in community and of community in self-hood than any other people of the ancient world; and simply because the tie that bound them had its origin not primarily in any voluntary association for mutual aid against their enemies, but in the consciousness of a Word of God that had set them under covenant to serve a purpose beyond their own and eternal. By it they were brought back repeatedly to a gracious and sovereign will at the center of their history: while Egypt fell, and Assyria, Babylon and Greece. Here in fact is to be found the inmost secret of their culture and of their uniqueness: not in law nor in ritual, but in their corporate relationship to a kingdom that was coming on this earth from beyond it.

It is of this corporate relationship as a Christian community that in the great ecumenical movements of Christendom we are becoming increasingly aware: not merely by reason of some imperative which has been thrust against us from without, buffeted as we are by the very circumstances of our life; nor merely by reason of the discoveries we have made of our common heritage; but more particularly by reason of that other and divine imperative from within which will not be stilled, rough handle it as we will. "That they all may be one; as thou, Father, art in me, and I in thee, that they also may be one in us: that the world may believe that thou hast sent me." What promises to come alive in our time is not so much a sentimental enthusiasm as it is a sobering realization, a shuddering sense of some fact that will no longer be flouted, lest the judgment begin again with the house of God. The unity of the Christian

[13] Jacques Maritain, *Education at the Crossroads* (New Haven: Yale University Press, 1943), p. 15.

Church is not something to be wrought with lowest-common-denominator techniques for the sake of expediency, in order to keep our civilization from destroying itself: it is something to be manifested in faith, whether our civilization decides to destroy itself or not. It belongs to the very character of that saving Word which is still God's saving deed in Christ Jesus, and is itself the reality which underlies our differences.

The reassertion of community

For the last quarter of a century and more, from the Conference at Edinburgh to the Conference in Amsterdam and the practical formation of the World Council of Churches during the war, that reality has been seeking expression. It has begun to recognize itself now as the only unbroken fellowship left in the world, bringing together races and nations, friend and foe, East and West: cutting across the lines of denominationalism; finding its wealth in variety; "if there be any trouble in any member," forsaking not one another, suffering with one another; holding fast its witness, but in love; cherishing its catholic functions of polity, of creed and sacrament, not so much as demonstrations of either unity or disunity, but as the manifold response of a living community, with the Church as its base, to the constructive grace of a living Christ Who is still the center of human life and human history.

In what other context can humanity validate itself again as human? In what other context can it ever learn to know itself as more than itself: not man as merely a child of nature, but man too as a child of God, and that less by creation than by redemption? In what other context can it ever come to understand that its allegiance is neither to this world nor to another, but to both worlds at once? That it is neither the architect nor the pawn of history, but the instrument itself as well as the arena of the kingdom of God? And that therefore to seek fulfillment in any community, whether of interest or of blood, of race or of soil, gathered around anything less than His kingdom, is to find the only possible outcome for itself not in salvation, but in that fatal apostasy, so characteristic of the modern world, toward something which is less than human!

5. THE CHURCH AS VEHICLE AND AGENT

So it is that the Christian Church, and the Christian Church alone, is set forth in history as the vehicle of the Divine life, and the nucleus of God's true humanity. It is an institution, but far more than an institution. Its function is forever creative. We who are of that fellowship are not a chosen people set here to live our lives alone. By the Word of God, and by His redeeming act, humanity is, and is one. We are set here to make actual that one-ness.

The centrality of the Church

I find myself completely bewildered by the self-announced experts who with some knowledge of the past and with some insight into the present situation, still think that Christianity and the Christian community can be dismissed. Granted that as Professor Shotwell has said, "the whole direction of Western progress has been away from the dominance of religion in cultural life, and toward what is called secularism,"[14] could anything be more obvious than that this very trend has carried

[14] James T. Shotwell, *Religious Revolution of Today* (Chicago: Houghton Mifflin Company, 1924), quoted by Walter M. Horton, *Can Christianity Save Civilization?* (New York: Harper & Brothers 1940), p. 17; which is itself a question, as G. Ernest Wright observes, that would never have occurred to any Old Testament prophet! *The Challenge of Israel's Faith* (Chicago: University of Chicago Press, 1944), p. 70.

within itself the seeds of its own dissolution? The movement from religion toward secularism has proved itself precisely the movement away from freedom, away from every man's right to be what he is capable of becoming, and directly toward slavery, which is the dire necessity that seems to rest in mankind today of becoming what it would not! The only hope we have lies not in continuance, but in reversal.

If we have not yet been beaten to our knees and driven back to the only foundation there is for any further catastrophe, it will be forthcoming, and it will not be late.

> Through these events [writes a Dutch churchman] God has opened a profoundly serious conversation with the Churches . . . about judgment, conversion, and renewal of life. The Churches are called to render account of their past and their present. From the Christian point of view there is nothing more dreadful than to imagine a Church emerging from this period without an inner change. One could hardly find any means more drastic than those which God is actually using to awaken the Church from the torture and contentment which in the past made it so unfaithful to its calling. The dechristianizing of the Western world which is only now revealing its true character and consequences is not only due to the defection of the world. It is due to the apostasy of the Church. May all this give us today a healthy fright![15]

It means that we have to be far more intent than we have ever been, congregations and denominations alike, not only on providing the secular life of humanity with some recognizable pattern of the Commonwealth of God, but far more intent too on shaping that secular life into some conformity with it. Any kind of defeatism at this point may be respectable enough

[15] W. A. Vissel 't Hooft, *op. cit.*, p. 33.

in theory; in fact, it can only be suicidal. There is no such thing as the salvation of men's souls that leaves out of its reckoning the whole corpus of the society that dwarfs them. It means that the Christian Church cannot snub Time in some apocalyptic frenzy for Eternity, or however impossible seems the kingdom of God on earth by-pass the corporate life of mankind for the sake of some dialectic deference to eschatology! Nothing is in the *eschaton*, writes Paul Tillich, which is not in history.[16] The corporate life of mankind is our business.

And there is plainly no hope for it apart from the Christian gospel. Ideals will no longer serve. They never were enough. Much of the mischief that has been wrought in the world has been wrought by our belief in them. We have tried to tear them away like flowers from the cultural soil in which they grew, only to find that what life they once had was a derived life. Their power was not in themselves but in the truth that gave them sustenance. Writes Dr. Hocking:[17]

> Values can survive only if, reaching out toward a metaphysical condition which their dream-shapes foreshadow, they *find it*. They need reality to climb on; they need a reality they can climb on. They want an independent source of standards, a mooring outside nature.

That reality, never to be exploited in the bare interest of survival yet forever to be apprehended at the very least and poorest as the ground of self-fulfillment, has been made flesh and blood in Jesus of Nazareth, who is the Christ of faith, standing at the precise point of intersection between the

[16] *The Journal of Religious Thought*, Autumn-winter, 1946. Vol. III, No. 1, p. 19.

[17] William E. Hocking, *Human Nature and Its Re-making* (New Haven: Yale University Press, 1923), p. 412. Quoted by John Baillie, *op. cit.*, p. 48.

immanent and transcendent sovereignty of the Eternal God and this "glory, gist and riddle of the world," which is the paradoxical nature of the human soul. In him "the infinite tension between the finite and the infinite" is carried backward into the "Ground of Being."[18] In him is revealed a Word which is not only irreversible judgment on human history but also indefatigable mercy toward human life and the whole creation, manifesting itself on the level of experience not first in order and "better behavior," but first in repentance and renewal. In him, in the mysteries of personal encounter, however you try to define or describe them, as men stand face to face with God, that vast reversal takes place of which Paul is forever talking: "Giving thanks unto the Father, which hath made us meet to be partakers of the inheritance of the saints in light: Who hath delivered us from the power of darkness, and hath translated us into the kingdom of his dear Son: In whom we have redemption through his blood, even the forgiveness of sins" (Col. 1:13). It is a forgiveness that is much more than forgiveness. Christ never stops with that. It is a forgiveness which if we allow it will fashion again within us the lost image of God, and in the power of God's Spirit constitute us the agents of His Eternal purpose.

The essential function

It may well be, therefore, that the one primarily relevant function which the Christian Church has to serve in our time is to pull these manifold secular problems of ours "this way round." In the lives of her members and in her own life she is to make clear again that "moral and political plasters" cannot be regarded as adequate treatment "for cultural earthquakes."[19]

[18] Paul Tillich, *op. cit.*, p. 26.
[19] V. A. Demant, in *The Christian Newsletter*, April 3, 1946.

Her task is neither by merely negative criticism, nor by any futile technique of detachment, but by realizing and offering herself as both the conscience of society and the continuing agent of God's design in human history, to establish as nearly as she can among sinful men through Word and Sacrament, through teaching and the shepherding of souls, through an aggressive evangelism, through works of serving love and her own incessant struggle against injustice and disorder, the kingdom of our Lord and of His Christ: a kingdom which may never be conceived as existing in any simple opposition to the kingdoms of this world, whether we think of the individual Christian or of the corporate life of society, but must ever be seen to exist in perpetual tension with them.

Surely here is a profounder commitment than any of which we used to dream; a heritage of such moment that to betray it further is to loosen the hold of Almighty God on generations yet unborn! There are even those who take it to mean that

> the traditional order in presenting the Gospel needs to be reversed. The prevailing practice is to start from God the Creator, tell men of the redemptive work of Christ and lead them by this path into the experience of the Holy Spirit. But since the content of our message has ceased to have any meaning for them, awakens no answering chord in their experience, the only thing to be done is to begin at the other end by showing them community in actual operation. Something new must enter into their experience before they can understand the Christian message. They must find in our churches in their hedgehog positions a more recognizable total witness. But not only in our churches. Christians must play their part in helping men to experience fellowship in the communities where they already are. When they have learned something of community life, and discover how easily and quickly natural community breaks

down and suffers defeat, the door is open to reveal Christ as the way of reconciliation and the revealer of God the Creator and of His purpose.[20]

6. THE CHURCH AS WORSHIPING COMMUNITY

This reorientation of the Christian community toward its proper and fundamental task can best be understood as the unfailing issue of all true worship, that outward and visible sign of an inward and spiritual grace (the *sobernost* of the Russian Orthodox) which is not alone the communion of the soul with God, but of God with man, and of men with one another in Him, of Whom and to Whom and through Whom are all things. Far beyond the expression of "personal piety," far beyond the "profession of Christian status" and fellowship how much farther beyond the techniques of autosuggestion and psychotherapy, the act of worship is "the corporate offering" of the Church herself by the Church,[21] a sacrifice of "penitence" and "consecration," which is her reasonable service, her inevitable response to the sacramental outpouring of God's own bounty in Christ Jesus.

Liturgy, thought and Sacraments

One is encouraged to hope that the widespread liturgical movement in modern Protestantism, with its determined attempt to evaluate afresh the tradition and practice of many centuries, may yet do more than record the nostalgic hunger for a sense of history which marks the end of every era, or represent the

[20] Dr. George MacLeod at the Cambridge Conference on Evangelism, reported in *Information Service*, April 27, 1946.

[21] Charles Clayton Morrison, *What Is Christianity?* (Chicago: Willett, Clark & Company, 1940), p. 226.

hysterical substitution of form for content which testifies to the bankruptcy of every faith: that it may mirror even now the slow recovery of a truer doctrine of the Church and the awakening into life of that central and creative experience which is Christian worship. Certainly there need be no loss of genuineness and sincerity as little by little we drop back into the quiet pools of memory not only our "chronic iconoclasm" but with it that dreadful spontaneity which culminated during the first four decades of the twentieth century in so much unintentional irreverence and trivial sentimentality!

Tending in the same direction should be set down too perhaps the virtual revolution which has taken place of recent years in theology: that swing away from a desiccated humanism, all too often no more than a kind of common sense, ethicized into half-a-dozen brands of prudential morality, and masquerading as religion, toward a more realistic interpretation of human nature, and so toward a rediscovery from within the Christian faith of what may be called Biblical Christianity. Such a sweeping turn of the tide should of its own momentum go far to rescue not only the forms of devotion but the sermon as well from its subjective, individualistic vagaries and reconstitute it as itself an act of worship, the authoritative Word not of man but of God, addressed to the community of believers from the very midst of that community, even as it was first heard there, that in it and through it a regnant Christ may have His own clear and unimpeded access to the bar of human souls, where He stands forever in judgment on His judge!

Further still, with no less eagerness and by a like token, may we look for the gradual restoration of the Sacraments at long last to their rightful place in the life of the Church. They are indeed "holy actions" and not "holy things." They are what we do, and in so far "we might perhaps as well do them elsewhere."[22] But they are more than that. They are, there within the living organism of the Christian Church, what "Christ says and does." Without His word and without His deed, water is "simply water, and no baptism"; the eating of bread and the drinking of wine, mere eating and drinking. Their efficacy to life and salvation consists not in the faith that apprehends them, but in Him by Whom through faith we are apprehended. They set no bounds nor limits to God's saving grace, but are nonetheless themselves the means of it. They are more than the bare symbols of a Presence that once was real. They are more even than the wistful behests of One who lived out his lonely years to a bitter death twenty centuries ago in Palestine, and to whom we now hold solemn memorial. They are Christ's gifts to His Church.

By means of them a man enters in and dwells where he is himself indwelt by "Jesus Christ the Lord," and where he

> mingles with the holiest of all the ages, children, like himself, of a mother solicitous and majestic, nurse of saints, yet mindful of her sinners, and keeping in her heart memories unspeakable so far back as the age of martyrs and the missions of the Apostles. When she takes him to her embrace, he ceases to be a casual atom of humanity: he becomes an heir of the ages, a citizen in the commonwealth of God; his name thence forward is entered in the vastest brotherhood ever known on earth, and written . . . in the book of life alone.[23]

So in his autobiography wrote William L. Sullivan, looking back on a youth from which he felt bound in later years to

[22] P. Carnegie Simpson, quoted by Charles Clayton Morrison, *op. cit.*, p. 229.

[23] William L. Sullivan, *Under Orders* (New York: Richard R. Smith, 1940), pp. 36 and 45. Cf. also pp. 139-169 for the "signatures," which not as Roman priest but as Unitarian minister he carried with him to the end!

break away; but never, would it seem, from what was to him still that communion of the faithful, that "realm of splendour, brilliant with its host of laureate victors, and loud with triumphant song."

7. THE CHURCH MILITANT AND TRIUMPHANT

Continuing struggle

Within the compass of so great a cloud of witnesses then is set this assembly of the first born to run with patience her appointed race. Hostility, resistance, suffering, death: these things she must expect, until Time plays itself out. Her warfare is not against flesh and blood, but against principalities, against powers, against the rulers of the darkness of this world, against spiritual wickedness in high places. Her task is not to restore: her task is to re-create; repentant herself, in the very moment of calling all men everywhere to repentance; cleansing and being cleansed; face to face as she knows herself to be through the ages with "the power and coming of our Lord Jesus Christ."

For that is always her reading of history. And never has it been easy. From the very beginning it has been a test of her faith to associate such a notion with Jesus of Nazareth. As a matter of fact, nobody did until after the resurrection. Then she knew beyond knowledge. Hers was to be the grim and ceaseless encounter between God and man just where human life keeps running into facts altogether tougher than it is, tougher than half-a-hundred proud and selfish and brutal things it has done, and liked doing, and wants to do again.

Ultimate victory

But she knew more. She knew that her long day was in very deed the Day of the Lord, and not simply her day: that something was at work in the world that never would let the ruins stay, unless people insisted on it; making toward a salvation not only individual and corporate but cosmic. She knew that she was not embarked on a hopeless crusade, that where grace abounds there might sin the much more abound! Whatever it is that is going on in our generation or in any other, the Christian gospel is certain that it means to salvage these lives of ours and great wide areas of human history with them. We are called to participate in a universal transformation which does not depend on signs. Nobody will prove it by any sign that things are getting better; and nobody will disprove it by any sign that things are getting worse. It depends on God, Whose nature it is to finish what long since He began and that nature doesn't change.

From nothing but this deep conviction has "the courageous testimony of the churches" of Europe sprung during these last most desolate years: from their discovery, as Dr. Warnshuis said on his return, that Christ reigns, not that He will reign. He is today the King of kings. Year in and year out the struggle seemed a very human struggle. But a Third had entered the contest. The world did not know it. Only the Church knew it. And knowing it, she spoke. It was inevitable that she should. Out of such despair alone could her hope be born. Not a hope that had dug itself up out of blueprints and charters. Unless we too can get away from the surface, we are done. The hope which saw clearly enough that we are done already—except for one live option still: a "re-created humanity" with the tragedy and the triumph of a cross at the heart of it.

The only kind of fulfillment Christianity has to offer in this earth comes by way of that gaunt and splendid thing, if ever we can learn to share it, that stands at the center of God's strange universe, holding life together, a compassion lean and strenuous that keeps staring at us. What the good Samaritan had in the story when he got down off his beast. It wasn't a good neighbor's policy, bent on winning friends and influencing people. He was not simply determined to do his duty that day; or set on going to heaven; or on improving the condition of the poor; or on making the world safe for travelers; or on establishing a just, endurable peace. There was something in him by the grace of God that was this much like God Himself. He was that sort. So he knelt there by the side of the road: until all you can hear in the story, as you lay your ear against it, is "the heart of the Eternal, most wonderfully kind."

Nor is the whole of it to be told here. This too faith knows. The sequel stands outside of history and beyond, when the Church militant on earth, her warfare accomplished, her iniquity pardoned, and the Church triumphant in heaven, the goodly fellowship of the redeemed that no man can number, shall be gathered in not without the whole creation, groaning now and travailing until He comes, "from the lowest material elements up to the angels and archangels," and made subject to that God Who hath indeed even now though we see it not, put all things under the feet of One to Whom every knee shall bow, of things in heaven, and things in earth, and things under the earth; and every tongue confess that Jesus Christ is Lord, to the glory of God the Father.

FURTHER READING

BAILLIE, JOHN. *What Is Christian Civilization?* New York: Charles Scribner's Sons, 1945.

FLEW, R. NEWTON. *Jesus and His Church.* New York: Abingdon-Cokesbury Press, 1938.

MORRISON, CHARLES CLAYTON. *What Is Christianity?* Chicago: Willett, Clark & Company, 1940.

VISSER 'T HOOFT, W. A. *The Wretchedness and the Greatness of the Church.* London: Student Christian Movement Press, Ltd., 1944.

The Nature of the Church. A Report of the American Theological Committee, of the Continuation Committee of the World Conference on Faith and Order. Chicago: Willett, Clark & Company, 1945.

3

THE CHRISTIAN HOPE OF A TRANSFIGURED WORLD

W. Norman Pittenger

1. Existential man: death, judgment and ultimate destiny as universal facts. 2. Christian presuppositions: man, history and the world of nature. 3. Beyond finitude: the world and eternity. 4. Christian affirmations: hell, heaven, resurrection, the "realization" of eschatology. 5. The faith and our life.

1. EXISTENTIAL MAN

The one inescapable and inevitable fact about every man is that he will die. It is in no sense morbid to face this and endeavor to come to terms with it; on the contrary, it is the measure of our humanity that we live daily as those who know that they are going to die, and hence can adjust themselves to the stupendous fact.

At no time in his history has man been content to consider death "a mere incident." Or, if this statement seems too extreme, at least we can affirm confidently that those who have thought longest and deepest about human life have never been content to dismiss death in a cavalier manner. They have seen it, rather, as a tremendous event which is to be approached respectfully, even fearfully; and if they have been in any sense religious, they would add that they must approach death faithfully, too.

In recent years, more especially, we have learned to take death with a high seriousness. Dismissal of the subject, or the assertion that "for those who believe there is no death," is all too readily taken to be, what it often is, an easy evasion of the awful reality itself. Death is *there*: the question is, can we come to terms with death?

But death is not there alone; it is there with a certain finality about it. For if it be true, on the one hand, that death is *the finality of life*, it is equally true, on the other hand, that death is *life in its finality*. That is, it is the distinctive fact which "conditions" and qualifies every human life. Man is the only animal, so far as we know, who is aware of his mortality and who may therefore meditate on the fact that he dies. He who has never pondered this truth and so "prepared for death" is by that token less than a true man. He is living under an illusion, out of touch with "things as they are."

As life in its finality, death introduces into our experience the fact of judgment. Judgment is a concept that many have sought to remove from our thinking about human life; like death, it often brings a somewhat unpleasant note into our discussions. But like death, it is a genuine and persistent factor. For what judgment means is that man is responsible for his life and must be prepared to give an account of his life, in the face of whatever ultimately determines and assesses true values in the universal scheme of things. It is not necessarily or essentially a future judgment; it is a present appraisal, day by day experienced by every man. It is the question, insistent in human life and thought, "How do I stack up, as against 'the way things are'?" It is a question which is as real for the communist as it is for the religious man. It is, in fact, the measure of man's moral responsibility and hence the determinant of his moral earnestness, precisely as awareness of death is the measure of his humanity.

Again, each man in every age is faced with two "destinies." He is given the possibility of moral choice, and hence of judgment; in the light of that judgment, he is offered the blessedness which comes from self-fulfillment or the disintegration which comes from self-destruction. If ever this truth were abundantly made clear in the literature of the world, it is to be found in Dostoevski's *Brothers Karamazov,* where Ivan, Aloysha and Dmitri are portrayed as caught in the dilemma of choice and by that fact judged, in their essential character, as *blessed* or *damned*—not by the arbitrary fiat of a *deus ex machina*, but by the ineluctable working of the nature of things, or that which above we have called "whatever ultimately determines and assesses true values in the universal scheme of things."

For each one of us, then, the final and exacting question which must be faced and answered is the question of our total mortal life, confronted as it is by appraisal in the light of the final truth about things, and in the light of that confrontation manifested as either possessed of some germ of blessedness which follows upon increasing realization of oneself, or (on the other hand) in process of such deterioration and disintegration as shall lead to complete and utter frustration and loss. Such a thinker as Heidegger confirms here the truth enunciated by Kierkegaard: Man is that mortal who is responsible for his actions and for his character, and as being thus responsible is damned or blessed.

2. CHRISTIAN PRESUPPOSITIONS

Now the Christian faith proposes to speak to man in this condition. It does not gloss over the facts, nor sentimentalize them, nor deny them. On the contrary, it is exactly here—in the uncertainty and even despair which come over man when he himself looks the facts squarely in the face—that the Christian gospel has its unique and special relevance. But before one can see what Christianity has to say to man, it is first of all necessary to understand the presuppositions with which Christian faith starts in its account of man, of history and of the natural world.

These suppositions may be summed up in the following statements: (1) Man, while a sinner, is capable of redemption and hence of glory. (2) History is not a meaningless meandering but a purposeful movement. (3) The natural world is good and will share in the total redemption. It will be useful to make some comments on each of them, so that we may have a rounded and well-balanced picture of the historic Christian view.

(1) *Man* is a sinner. This is a given fact of our experience, requiring only a little observation and introspection to become a horrible realization in our mind and thought. The doctrine of the Fall and Original Sin, while the historical moment or actual detail may be pictorial, tells the truth about man. He is a sinner, fallen from grace; he is "not able of himself to help himself." Even if we cannot accept the notion of man's total depravity, as this has commonly been interpreted, we can agree wholly with the insight behind that notion—namely, that man, existentially known, is so "far gone from original righteousness" that "he is not able to stand up-

right." Both man's situation and man's present nature are corrupted.

The truth about man, as Christianity sees it, is that while he was created "in the image of God," he is now in a state of spiritual insufficiency so pervasive and so disturbing that he is unable to live truly as a man, much less live as a son of God. In the divine intention and plan, he was made for the fulfillment of himself in God, with a free relationship with his Creator: in actual fact, he has lost the capacity for communion with God in such free and open fashion, while in his natural human state he is disorganized and maladjusted. As the scholastics used to say, he is not only deprived of supernatural grace; he is also *vulneratus in naturalibus*, wounded in the natural parts of his being. In consequence, he is possessed by a drive or tendency which leads him to live for less than ultimate goods, which makes him rest content with the immediately attainable goals of human endeavor, which perverts his better impulses and prevents his seeing life or anything else "steadily and whole." That is man as he is.

But the doctrine of the resurrection, and with it the Christian hope of a transfigured world, makes it impossible for Christian faith to rest there. The recognition of man's sinfulness seems to be about all that some contemporary thinkers, Christian and non-Christian, can manage to encompass. The genuine Christian picture, however, must go beyond this. If the first volume, in our story of man, is about his sin, the second volume must always be about redemption. For man can be redeemed. Man's possibilities are tremendous. He was created "in the image and likeness of God"; the likeness, as St. Iraenaeus says, is lost, but the image remains. Man still has the capacity, but he lacks the power, to be "righteous." In other words, the actual "conforming to Christ's humanity" is the goal; the *possibility* of such conforming is an article of faith. Christ's perfected human nature, which is true manhood, is for us men a possibility by adoption and grace.

Thus when we have admitted all that we must admit concerning man's helplessness, we must go on to affirm all that we can affirm concerning man's perfectability. It is not correct to say, as some may have said, that *in this present world and under these present circumstances* man may be perfected. It is entirely correct to hope that by God's grace in response to man's humble faith, man can come eventually to the perfection which is proper to him. That will be "in heaven"; but the belief in it gives us courage and confidence as we are called to deal with men in their miserable wickedness and perversion. No Christian can despair of any man, for each man is "a sinner for whom Christ died" and therefore "can work out his salvation with fear and trembling, for it is God that worketh in him both to will and do of his good pleasure." This is the position of central historical Christianity.

It is largely because the Christian "hope of heaven" has faded from the living thought of Christian theologians that we have been offered the "depression theologies" of recent years. A silly optimism about man, in the fashion of the "late liberals," is not Christian; but neither is a total pessimism about him, in the fashion of some of the "neo-orthodox." It is probably the case, indeed, that the loss of a conviction about man's "heavenly hope" is the cause of the quite literally *hopeless* view of man that is taken. When man's possibilities are limited to this infinite existence, his possibilities are indeed limited. There is little enough here to give ground for much belief in the poor human creature, frustrated, conditioned, "cabined, cribbed, confined." In a word, if we do not believe in heaven, we shall not believe in man.

This Christian assertion of man's possibility is expressed in various ways in the several theologies of the Church. The Protestant world has more frequently stated it in terms of eschatology; it is a hope, the first reflections of which are experienced today. Catholic thought, in all its forms (Eastern, Roman, Anglican), has tended to put it in more metaphysical language: the seed of redemption is planted at baptism and grows in the garden of the Church until it reaches its full flower in heaven; it is a real impartation of divine nature that is made to the believer, whether he be a child or adult. In either instance, however, the basic assertion remains. Man, though a sinner, is redeemed in Christ; man, remaining a sinner, may grow in grace even now; man, sin being done away, may realize his proper perfection, "to glorify God and enjoy him forever" in the perfect vision which is heaven.

(2) *History* is not a meaningless meandering but a purposeful movement. The belief in progress, so popular and so cheap, was the secular substitute for the Christian conviction of purposeful movement in history. "The far-off divine event" to which the Christian looks is not the end of a long temporal development, although that is included in it; it is a trans-historic reality in which each historic event and the sum total of historical change finds its present and its future goal. "The increasing purpose" is not automatic progress through the rolling years, but a divinely guided movement in which each moment counts and in which a total significance is extracted from history by a God who is above history but intimately concerned in its infinite variety and content.

Mother Julian of Norwich relates that, in a vision, she was shown the entire creation as "a little hazel-nut." She asked how it could continue in existence, so tiny was it in relation to the vastness of God. The answer came that it continued "because God made it, because God Loved it; because God keeps it." Those three statements sum up that which one would say, Christianly, about the historical process. God is the Creator of the world—that is, He sustains its every event and is the Ultimate Cause behind all causation. God loves the world—He has entered into it to bring His cherishing care as an intimate fact of experience to every man and thereby to redeem the world from triviality and frustration. God keeps it —there is a purpose in the world, seen by St. Paul in his great chapter in Romans: "the manifestation of the sons of God." Whatever may be the remoter intention of God in the awe-inspiring stretch of space and time, this purpose stands sure in our human historic sphere; and toward this, God works and man may, in some degree, co-operate.

It is only when automatic development is substituted for this idea that we come to an absurdity. The Christian can see how it is that human history is not simply an escalatorlike movement toward some supreme finite goal; such a conception overlooks the fact of sin and its root in original sin, with its consequence in the strange truth that as history represents a growth in the possibility of the better, so it also represents a discovery on man's part of more subtle ways of sinning. But it is only when one has accepted Christ, risen and ascended, as the *meaning* of history, that one can be delivered from utter pessimism or puerile optimism. In that moment of insight, one can see that the purpose of God in the historical realm is twofold. It is to extract the good from each moment and from each event; it is to work toward such a completion of the entire process that in the end God can behold it to have been good in that entirety.

This must involve the confidence that God can overrule even the worst, so that it may serve His good. The demonic can never become satanic, as Tillich puts it; but the very demons—those drives toward self-contained and cancerous realization—can be made, by the medicine of the Cross, to serve God's purpose. Even the murder of God the Son can be turned to good; Mr. T. S. Eliot's phrase puts it well "And yet, we call this Friday *good*." *O felix culpa*, says the Holy Saturday liturgy in the Western Church, describing man's fall in Adam, *O felix culpa quae meruit tantam redemptionem.* For if the history of the human race is from one point of view the story of the discovery of more subtle ways of sinning, it is also the story of God's incredibly cherishing love, that finds ways in which even man's sinning can be made the material for a greater sanctity. Like a sculptor who can turn an artisan's mistaken chiseling into a lovely figure, God's purpose can—and does—make history meaningful even when man has done his utmost to pervert it.

(3) *The natural world* is essentially good and will share in the total redemption. As against all Manichaean or dualistic philosophies, Christianity insists that the world of things is neither evil nor doomed to total extinction. The world is good in its creation by God; its imperfections and perversions, somehow present and at work as the world now stands, will be eradicated by God's gracious action, so that the rich range of nature may be transformed and changed into a spiritualized but real instrument for the divine purpose.

The Eastern Church's theologians have much to teach us about this matter. For them, the whole cosmos is to be redeemed; everything in it, from the very dirt at our feet up to the loveliest configurations and harmonies, will have its place in the redemption. There is no reason, therefore, to fear or hate "dirt" or "matter" or "things." They may be misused; they can be abused; in themselves they cannot fulfill their proper end. But they are "good stuff" for God's building, since He made them; they are never to be despised or rejected. It is interesting in this connection to compare two literary men who have lately been converted to religion. Mr. Aldous Huxley has come to some sort of quasi Buddhist mysticism, dismissing the finite temporal sphere as illusory and unimportant. In consequence, he has not yet been delivered from that contempt for the body and from that fear of sex which was found in his preconversion days and now reappears in his recent novels such as *Time Must Have a Stop.* On the other hand, in his *Christmas Oratorio*, Mr. Wystan Auden, who has been converted to Orthodox Christianity, writes superbly and lovingly of the possibilities of the natural world, and speaks tenderly although critically of man the sexual being. The practical result shows that the Orthodox point of view, which Mr. Auden accepts, is the theological justification of the *essentially Christian* position, which he takes.

For Christian faith, the resurrection of the body has never meant "the resuscitation of relics" but the transfiguration of the material body into "the body of glory" which can fittingly serve as spiritual vehicle for the redeemed soul of man. The doctrine of the resurrection of the body provides, too, a clew to the destiny which awaits the natural world. Indeed, the two may be very closely related; it is the writer's opinion that they are, and that Christian faith has held the two ideas together precisely for this reason. The natural world is good and can be redeemed; man is to be raised from the dead by the power of God and live in newness of life with Christ. In some fashion, far beyond our power to describe or even imagine, the whole creation will be changed so that, as a whole, it may serve as "the body of God." To be afraid of that phrase in this particular connection is to be afraid of the Christian doctrines of creation and redemption; to use it in any other connection is likely to suggest pantheism or even monism.

It may be asked, naturally, what will be the relationship of the present world of chemistry and physics to the transformed cosmos. The answer to this question is that the material world in the strict sense of unmodified *stuff* will be related to the "new heavens and the new earth" by the fact of continuity but not by the fact of sheer identity. As the risen body is not the same thing as the body that was placed in the grave, but is a "spiritual body," continuous with the "natural body" and bearing the marks of that which the natural body experienced; so the renewed creation will be continuous with and determined by what went on in the world of chemistry and physics. In other words, the redeemed cosmos will be, in truth, *what the world means to God*, in terms of what it has been and has done. If the question is further pressed, one can only respond, "We speak concerning a mystery." But we must hasten to add that unless something of this sort be true, the creation itself is rendered meaningless excepting as a stage for *man's* redemption—and here is a religious anthropocentrism as radically wrong and as dangerous as the secular anthropocentrism from which the Copernican revolution delivered us.

In the *De Divisione Naturae*, Erigena has grandly developed the theme that the entire created order is to return to God and find its fulfillment in Him. As the creation came forth through the operation of the Word of God, so it returns by the operation of the Word. The microcosmic instance of this is the "process of salvation" for men; the macrocosmic instance is the *whole* of things. The agent in each case is Christ, the Word of God; God the Father is Alpha and Omega, Beginning and End; the Holy Spirit is the power of God who is life-giver in the great movement. With whatever exaggeration Erigena wrote, his insight appears to be fundamentally that of the great doctors of the Church and of St. Paul himself in the New Testament, notably in Romans and Colossians.

Such a cosmic setting for, and involvement in, redemption gives the Christian faith a sweep and range, a universal character and a vast inclusiveness, that saves it from all charges of parochialism or provincialism or anthropocentrism. Perhaps it is the truth which the Nicene Creed affirms when it refers to Christ the Word as him "by whom all things were made," and then goes on to say of him that "his Kingdom shall have no end," for we believe also in "the resurrection of the dead, and the life of the world to come."

3. BEYOND FINITUDE

Two contemporary phrases come to mind when one thinks of the subject of this essay. One of these is simply the title of a popular novel of a few years ago. When one hears a discussion of the tremendous value of Christianity, its promise of abundant life, its giving of a meaning to our present-day existence, its substitution of an integrated and forgiven personality for a broken and sin-ridden one, one always thinks of that title, *All This and Heaven Too.* For Christianity offers everything that is good and helpful for this world, and heaven too. And if the phrase is forgotten, the whole picture is out of proportion.

The second phrase is a popular slang expression, used by young folk and some of their elders to convey the idea that something is superlatively good and splendid, *and* slightly mysterious: "It's out of this world." Precisely. For whatever is superlatively good and splendid, and slightly mysterious—and the superlatively good and splendid always *is* slightly mysterious—is "out of this world," beyond this world and what it contains and offers in itself, although operative in and through this world in a partial and limited fashion. It is the sense of "the more" in our life and experience which somehow compels us to see that even the best and most utopian mundane existence could never exhaust or adequately manifest "what God hath prepared for them that love him." And no statement of the Christian gospel is really valid which lacks the eschatological note, refusing to see that gospel's implications for eternity by reason of a preoccupation with human events alone.

This world and eternity

It is patently true that for many years there was a tendency both within the Christian Church and on the part of outside observers to make the faith "otherworldly" in an extreme sense. This tendency was parodied by the Communists in their song about the capitalists *and* the religionists who promised "pie in the sky when you die" by-and-by.

A desirable reaction to this nonsense, however, forced others in the Christian Church to the opposite extreme. Christianity, for them, was so utterly "this-worldly" that its gospel seemed almost to be exhausted either in the promise of a personal and present enrichment of life or in the imperative to build up in the not too distant future a society in which "abundant life" could be guaranteed to all men. Today, one imagines, the latter tendency rather than the former is still the stronger of the two. Despite the rediscovery of "the politics of eternity" by our theologians, the popular Christian mind, especially in Anglo-Saxon and predominantly Protestant countries, leans toward a view of the Christian faith which is concerned pre-eminently with better relations among men, classes, races and nations, based on a readjusted personality in each believer.

Yet the slightest acquaintance with the New Testament, let alone the history of Christian thought in the ages since that time, should make it perfectly plain that an essential ingredient of the Christian complex has been a due recognition of the fact that "we are strangers and pilgrims" in this world; that the world itself is what John Keats called a "vale of soul-making"; and that the Christian religion contains a *hope*, which is that this world and all that is in it, including man himself, is to be transfigured and changed. There is more in man and there is more in the world "than meets the eye" of natural man; as St. Paul saw, "the whole creation groaneth and travaileth in pain" until it shall "be delivered from the bondage of corruption into the glorious liberty of the children of God." Or, as he puts it in Colossians, the reconciliation in Christ affects not only man, but "all things . . . whether they be things in earth or things in heaven."

The world as a whole, then, is the creation of God and is included in His total purpose. And since that purpose, in view of the corruption which has entered into the finite order, now involves redemption and reintegration on the new level which in Christ has been inserted into the creation, the world as a whole is included in this vast process by which all things return to God. The developed theology of the Church has worked this out in connection with the dogma of the Trinity, saying that as the creation was made by the Father through the agency of the Eternal Word and by the power of the Holy Spirit, so the creation returns to God, in *adunatio* or final union, by the Holy Spirit through Him by whom all things were made, the Lord Jesus Christ who is the Eternal Word now enfleshed and dwelling in His Church. This means that in a very real and vital sense the full and proper meaning of "Church" is the redeemed and transformed cosmos, from the lowest material elements up to the angels and archangels.

Admittedly it is a little difficult for us today, more prosaic in mind and less given to use imagination or even imagery in our theology, to grasp this grand scheme. Yet there can be no doubt that it has been held by the greatest Christian "doctors" from the days of St. Irenaeus and St. Augustine. The main stream of historic Christianity has never been content with a picture of our religion which confined salvation to man himself and excluded the natural world, nor with a notion of redemption which was so narrowly interested in making life here and now a meaningful reality that it forgot man's ultimate destiny "beyond the flaming ramparts of space and time."

Nor should it be forgotten that this conception of man and his world, in their ultimate destiny and final significance has been expressed, normally, in worship more than in theology. The central work of the Christian Church, historical Christianity has always maintained, is the worship of God. The ancient versicle and response from the Office of Compline puts this: "Let us bless the Father and the Son and the Holy Ghost: Let us praise and exalt him forever." The chief means whereby this worship is performed is the Lord's Supper, which (as the catechism in the Anglican Book of Common Prayer puts it) is "the continual remembrance of the sacrifice of the death of Christ." Now that rite, which is the characteristic expression of Christianity—summing up, as St. Thomas Aquinas declared, "the whole of our salvation"—is marked in all liturgies, whether traditional or "free," by the offering of the whole of man and his entire world back to God, in union with the pleading of the death of Christ on Calvary. There is more in the Eucharist than oblation, but the sacrament is always celebrated, in St. Paul's phrase, as "showing forth the Lord's death, till he come." The Eucharist is both cosmic and eschatological in its significance. The two ideas are beautifully stated in the usual Western version of the *Sanctus*: "Holy, Holy, Holy, Lord God of Hosts. Heaven and earth are full of thy glory. Blessed is he that cometh in the name of the Lord: Hosanna in the highest."

4. CHRISTIAN AFFIRMATIONS

We have seen that historically no Christian thinker has ever been content with a picture of man which failed to include an ultimate destiny greater than his span of years on this planet. Attempts to substitute for this conviction of ultimate destiny some such notion as "social immortality" or "persistence by influence" have always met with strong opposition. In the central stream of Christian theology, *death, judgment, heaven* and *hell* have played a real part in the picture of man and his ultimate destiny.

The Christian faith affirms that man's action and character in this world have a determining influence upon that which will happen to him. He will not, in any case, suffer annihilation; the question, rather, is what sort of "future" is before him?

Hell

The first possibility is that he shall so terribly fail, because of his ignorance and impotence, to do God's will that he will be unable to enjoy the vision of God; hence he will be *deprived* of that vision and will continue to exist, in some sense, apart from it. This is hell—by definition, the absence of God. We have said this is the *first* possibility because the tendency today would be the other way round; man is so sure of heaven, many would be inclined to feel, that hell may readily be forgotten. Quite the contrary, though, for the traditional theology of the Church. Hell is always a real and live possibility, although the Church's doctors have (so far as one is aware) consigned no particular person to that fate. If one believes in God, in anything like the full Christian sense (in which God is taken to be the ultimate moral Reality, upon whom all else depends for its existence), and at the same time believes in man as a free and responsible moral agent, the possibility of willful alienation from God and persistence in that alienation is a required *possibility*. Further, if God be love in its profoundest depth and at the same time the respecter of my moral freedom, He could never *force* me to love Him; he could only *win* me to Him by love, and I could always decline His solicitations.

Heaven

The opposite possibility to alienation from God is the possibility of the enjoyment of God which is called in classical theology "the beatific vision" and in popular thought is probably what is meant when "heaven" is mentioned.

In the Roman, Eastern and Anglican theologies, the existence of an intermediate state is taught. Here, it is claimed, provision is made after death for such purgation from sin and for such growth in divine favor as shall fit those who are heaven-bound "to behold the King in his beauty." The Protestant theologies have *tended*, in most instances, to omit this notion, partly in reaction from Roman Catholic extremes and even superstitions in the late Middle Ages. In recent years, however, one notices among Protestants something of a return to some such idea and to prayers for the departed—a practice which is a vital element in all Catholic piety.

Here if anywhere the religious imagination has been at work; the pictures of heaven, whether they be the grand vistas of Dante's *Paradiso* or the homely fields of *Green Pastures* or merely the conventional "I'll be with those I love," are at best symbolic and suggestive. The only certain definition of heaven is that it means enjoying God and all things which are God's in God. That enjoyment is no passive "basking in divinity" but the superabundant bliss of a full realization of self in God and for God, as it is also a life by God and with God. "When I wake up after his likeness, I shall be satisfied," says the Psalmist; and it is part of Christian hope to add, again with the Psalmist, "at thy right hand are pleasures for evermore."

Resurrection

A friend once remarked, too cleverly for accuracy, that "Christianity knows nothing about the immortality of the soul, but it is all about the resurrection of the body." Reinhold Niebuhr has lately been contending, on the whole rightly, that the resurrection of the body is a richer conception than the immortality of the soul for it guarantees the value and preservation of the totality of personality rather than of some supposedly "spiritual" fragment of man's life.

The complexity and even confusion of Christian eschatology is precisely in the fact that Christianity attempts to bring into some sort of unity the Greek notion of "immortality" and the Hebrew idea of "resurrection." The tension between these two conceptions has been "rich and fruitful" (in von Hügel's favorite phrase); perhaps the clew to the confusion in the resulting picture is that the Greek tended to think of the "soul" as man's individuating principle, while the Hebrew took the "body" to be the distinguishing factor. In each case the purpose was to maintain that "the-whatever-it-is-that-makes-man-a-man" was not destroyed at death, but survived in the fullest sense.

The Christian faith in the "resurrection of the body," however, goes beyond this. It insists that *God* is the principal actor here. Man may be naturally immortal, but only by God's free and gracious gift does he have that victory over death which gives him "the life that was with the Father and was manifested unto us." Life-in-Christ is the meaning of resurrection; the body of our glory begins to grow in us here and now, while it is wonderfully raised into God's new life "when we shall all be changed." Each shall have his own expressive medium for his own personality, his "resurrection body," and all shall be one in Christ, by whose rising-again the promise of our risen life is revealed.

To try to break down this rich imagery into literal conceptual language is both impossible and absurd. As it stands it is evocative and indicative of meaning. When it is reduced to dull prose it loses that meaning. But because it is imagery it is not thereby untrue; it is, on the contrary, true in the deepest sense. In the word popular today, it is *myth*, which does not tell lies but speaks truth that words in themselves can never define nor confine but to which they can at best significantly point. A reading of chapter 15 of I Corinthians will do more to intimate, in a vivid image, the meaning of the doctrine of the resurrection of the body than all theological treatises put together. But that meaning will be lost entirely if from our reading of that magnificent passage we seek to work out a neat set of ideas which we then characterize as "the Pauline view."

The faith in the resurrection is faith in Christ, or rather faith in the God who united humanity in Christ and raised humanity "from the bondage of corruption" to the right hand of God. Therefore Christ's humanity, raised from the dead, is the earnest of the final redemption of all men and their world. "He is the first fruits of them that sleep"; but he is also that one concerning whom here and now it may be said, "As in Adam all die, even so in Christ shall all be made alive." That is, resurrection is not a future hope or expectation alone; it is a present reality for Christians. The Christian life *is* realized eschatology; it is the "end of the ages" present in the immediacy of our own time and experience. "The resurrection-life" is both here and to come; it is a present fact and a future hope, the fact of life in Christ in his Body which is the Church and the hope of glory "when this mortal shall have put on immortality, this corruptible incorruption." Meanwhile and always it is the part of the Christian to say, "It is not I, but Christ in me." That living in Christ as Christ lives in the faithful *is* "our hope of glory."

The "realization" of eschatology

The plain man has a right to ask what this means in the terms of ordinary life. To that question I should reply that it means a humble and faithful membership in the One Holy Catholic and Apostolic Church, which for faith *is* Christ's divine life in our present world. It means a courageous trust in the God who raised Jesus from the dead and by that act restored to men confidence and hope. It means detachment from, yet closest concern for and action in, the world. It means supremely the adoration of the eternal God who is our refuge and strength—the God who in Christ has become our redeemer. It means the implementation of that adoration in daily experience so that the believer becomes an "other Christ" to those who as yet do not know him. And in it all, through it all, the Christian believes, lives, worships and acts as one whose life is "in the heavenlies"; as one whose belief, worship and action are never frustrated by the denials and limitations of this temporal world, since he does not "put all his eggs in one basket." It is "all this—and heaven, too."

5. THE FAITH AND EXISTENTIAL MAN

And now we come full circle. Man is the animal who dies, who knows that he dies. Man is the responsible animal, held accountable before the ultimate court of appeal, "things as they really are." Man is the creature who may know blessedness in self-fulfillment of his potentialities or damnation in self-destruction. But for Christian faith there is more to be said. For Christian faith man is also the sinner, guilty of defection from the God who made him and hence incapable of raising himself to any significant level of life. He is set in a world in which purposes, far beyond his comprehension, are being effected; yet, with all his imperfection and perversity, and in spite of his "littleness," he is intended to have a place and part in those purposes, partially fulfilling them here and finding his only fruition in them beyond this world of becoming. Nonetheless, the world itself is in essence good, and in the divine purpose it will be redeemed, as will man himself, into the richness of meaning which God has from all eternity planned as the goal "to which the whole creation moves."

So the fact that we die opens up for the Christian the understanding of finite life as at every moment meaningful but yet never exhausting all the meaning that it can possess. He is too big for this world; he requires eternity. The fact that we are judged opens up for the Christian the understanding that he is a responsible being, whose moral integrity and high seriousness count enormously in the scheme of things. He is to respond to his high calling as "son of God" in such fashion that his responsibility becomes that of one who is *needed* to complete "the scheme of things." The fact that we may enjoy blessedness opens up for the Christian the understanding that "God has set eternity in his heart," so that his final resting place can be in God alone; while it also validates and enriches the daily round by suffusing our mundane life with "bright shoots of everlastingness"— or, in prosaic idiom, redeeming the time by giving its every moment the guarantee of an eternal value. Finally, the fact that we by our selfishness and pride are in peril of self-destruction opens up for the Christian the understanding that it is only as he turns from self-regarding thought and action to the service of "the all-great and the all-loving" that he is delivered from frustration and ultimate despair and given "the glorious liberty of the children of God."

Further Reading

TAYLOR, A. E. *The Christian Hope of Immortality*. London: J. Heritage, The Unicorn Press, 1938.

BAILLIE, JOHN. *And the Life Everlasting*. New York: Charles Scribner's Sons, 1933.

NIEBUHR, REINHOLD. *The Nature and Destiny of Man* (Vol. 2). New York: Charles Scribner's Sons, 1945.

HALL, F. J. *Eschatology*. New York: Longmans, Green and Company, 1922.

VON HÜGEL, F. *Eternal Life*. Edinburgh: T. and T. Clark, 1912.

PART II. The Church and The World

CHAPTER IV

The Church and Christian Society Today in the Perspective of History

KENNETH SCOTT LATOURETTE

CHAPTER V

The Responsibility of the Church for Society

RICHARD NIEBUHR

CHAPTER VI

The Limitations of the Church

JOHN C. BENNETT

4

THE CHURCH AND CHRISTIAN SOCIETY TODAY IN THE PERSPECTIVE OF HISTORY

Kenneth Scott Latourette

1. Introduction: the issues at stake. 2. The amazing record: inauspicious beginnings, the youth of Christianity. 3. The three criteria of Christian advance. 4. The Christian tide: recessions and advance. 5. The present age: dangers and progress. 6. The outlook: the place of the United States, expansion, unity, Protestant ascendancy and change. The Church and the world.

1. THE ISSUES AT STAKE

How does the Christianity of today appear when seen against the perspective of its past? As a factor in the world is it advancing or receding? Is it growing or dwindling in its effect upon mankind? Does history afford any way of gauging the future of Christianity? What progress, if any, has Christianity made toward bringing the world to its ideal? What is the relation of Christianity to the great social and intellectual forces which are shaping the world of our day? Is it at all modifying them, and, if so, to what extent? In what direction is Christianity moving? Judged in the light of the past and of current trends, what forms of Christianity are to be dominant in the immediate future? Upon the churches of what country or countries is the main burden for the Christian achievement of the coming generation to rest? These are questions which are of prime importance for the Church and for all earnest Christians as they endeavor to make their faith count to the full in the years which lie ahead.

2. THE AMAZING RECORD

Inauspicious beginnings

First of all we must realize that the spread of Christianity is the most amazing and thought-provoking phenomenon in history. At the outset the outlook for the faith was far from promising. Christianity sets impossibly high standards. Its adherents are commanded, in contrast with impelling drives of men, not to be anxious about food or clothing, to be absolutely honest, to love their enemies, to forgive until seventy times seven, and to be perfect as God is perfect. The founder of Christianity had only a brief public career. He wrote no book and seems to have given little or no thought to perpetuating his influence through an organization. His death at the hands of his enemies was, from the standpoint of worldly prudence, needless. On the first Good Friday night it seemed futile. The little band of friends was disheartened. One of their number had betrayed their Lord and another had denied him. When, in response to the resurrection, the group reassembled, it was only one of several Jewish sects and presumably the weakest of them. The faith with these apparently quite impracticable ideals and this very discouraging beginning in numbers and influence, has become the major force in the history of mankind. This astonishing record poses and sheds light on the most profound questions which man can ask about the nature of the universe and of the human drama. These we cannot discuss in so brief a paper as this must be. However, this past renders the appraisal of the present condition of Christianity and the attempt to determine the direction in which its embodiment, the Church, is moving, basic to any understanding of the current world scene.

The youth of Christianity

We must next appreciate the fact that Christianity is still young. This assertion may seem surprising. Has not Christianity been present for more than nineteen centuries? Is not the Church the oldest existing institution with a continuous history? Yet compared with the length of years that mankind has been on the earth, Christianity's course has been brief. Contrasted even with the time that human civilization has been developing, perhaps fifteen to twenty thousand years, Christianity has thus far had only a short life. More significantly, as we are to say in the succeeding paragraphs, Christianity bears many of the earmarks of youth. If one considers mankind as a whole, it is still spreading rapidly. In most lands Christians are only a minority, but in many nations, especially non-Occidental peoples, they are growing in numerical strength. The Church has only begun to fulfill the commission of its founder to the Apostles to teach all men to observe all that he commanded them. Its most striking advance toward attaining that ideal has been not in the distant past but in the past century and a half. Christianity appears to be gaining momentum and to be only at the outset of its task. In many ways and in many lands it is displaying great vigor. Indeed, if this interpretation is true, we are in the early days of the Church.

In the third place, as we survey its past we become aware that Christianity has gone forward by successive pulsations. To take the full and accurate measure of Christianity in history, we must see the course of the faith against the background of the entire human race, and not merely against one or another of the segments of mankind. As we adopt this world-embracing perspective, we become aware that, most amazingly, Christianity has been a growing force in the life of the race.

3. THE CRITERIA OF CHRISTIAN ADVANCE

As criteria for judging the advance or recession of the faith we have the geographic extent of Christians at successive stages, the varying degrees to which Christianity gives rise to new movements and the effect of Christianity upon mankind.

The first of these criteria can readily be determined with a kind of rough accuracy. For almost any century we can know approximately the boundaries within which Christian communities were to be found and beyond which they did not extend. Never, not even today, can we discover the precise totals of those who at any given moment profess and call themselves Christians. Yet usually we can know the majority of the peoples, tribes, and cities in which Christians are numerous. Obviously here is an important measuring stick for determining advance or recession.

The second criterion, the emergence of new movements from Christianity, is also fairly easily applied. Christianity, like other religions, seems to vary in vigor. At one stage of its history it appears to be static and to be giving birth to nothing new. At another period great creative spirits spring from it.

They produce theological systems which show intellectual power and deep insight. Or they inspire others and from them arise new religious orders, denominations or societies. Or they expressed themselves in kindling hymns and contagious works of devotion. Usually these varying indications of life are fairly contemporaneous. Francis of Assisi and Dominic, the founders respectively of the Order of Brothers Minor and the Order of Preachers, each spanned the close of the twelfth and the beginning of the thirteenth century. From both orders in the first flush of their youthful power came outstanding theologians, notably Thomas Aquinas from the Dominicans. The sixteenth century saw Luther, Calvin, Ignatius Loyola, and the movements, theologies, works of devotion and hymns which issued from the impulses in which they were outstanding figures. The nineteenth century witnessed the appearance of more orders and societies in the Roman Catholic Church than had any one century before it. It was an era of even greater activity in Protestantism, with the emergence of scores of new movements, thousands of new societies, widespread religious awakenings, a flood of hymns, and theologies which shaped thought for generations.

The third criterion, the effect of Christianity upon mankind as a whole, is far more difficult to gauge than are the other two. This is partly because we cannot always ascertain the precise share which Christianity has in a particular aspect of culture. Usually we can know when Christianity is a factor in producting a particular movement or institution. Frequently, however, we cannot determine how large a factor it has been. We can prove it has been important in the foundation of the earliest colleges and universities in the United States. How great a role it plays in American university life of today can probably not be established. We are aware that Christianity has contributed to the rise and growth of democracy, but we cannot demonstrate that it has been the major source. We can adduce reasons for the hypothesis that from Christianity came the initial impulse for the development of the scientific method. We have not found evidence which will clinch the argument.

However, in some movements the dominance of the Christian element is clear. Such have been the beginnings of the antislavery agitation in Great Britain and the United States, the reduction of hundreds of languages to writing and the foundations of the modern professions of medicine and nursing in China.

Still greater difficulty in estimating the effect of Christianity is created by the fact that the chief influence is upon persons, whether as individuals or collectively in society. Persons, so the Christian confidently declares, have only the small beginnings of their life this side the gate of death. The ultimate effect of Christianity, therefore, we can never really know until we ourselves have made that great transition.

4. THE CHRISTIAN TIDE

As we employ these three criteria the great pulsations in the advance of Christianity become apparent.

Initial advance

The first covered approximately the five centuries immediately after Christ. In these years Christianity won at least the nominal allegiance of the vast majority of the population of the Roman Empire and spilled over the borders of that realm into adjacent countries. For magnitude this achievement was without previous parallel in the history of religion. Yet we must remember that the Roman Empire embraced only a small section of the earth's surface and that several high cultures and great masses of people, notably in China and India, were not included in it and were as yet either entirely untouched or only slightly affected by Christianity. In these five centuries Christianity brought into being the Church, gave rise to Christian theology, liturgies and a huge literature, and stimulated the beginnings and spread of Christian monasticism. It also largely eliminated most of its rivals, molded the ideals and the morals of its adherents, modified the amusements and contributed to the decline of slavery in the Mediterranean Basin.

This initial achievement to a large degree determined the cultural association of Christianity from that time until the present. By it Christianity became so closely connected as to be almost identified with what we usually term Occidental civilization. In the course of the centuries it profoundly modified that culture and in turn was influenced by it. The subsequent spread of the faith has been chiefly in connection with the expansion of the West.

Yet Christianity did not prevent the collapse of the Empire which was the scene of its first major triumph. Its outstanding creations were in the realm of religion. While it brought into being the Church, Christian theology, literature and worship, strove to lift its adherents to a higher plane of moral and spiritual life, and modified some phases of culture, most of the main currents of life outside religion were but slightly affected. When Christianity was born, Greco-Roman civilization was already suffering from basic disorders. Christianity was not the cause of the illnesses which brought that ancient world to its end, but it did not cure them.

Threatened existence

The disintegration of the Roman Empire and its culture threatened the very existence of Christianity. Christianity had become identified with the Roman realm and now that realm was breaking up. For about four and a half centuries, or approximately from A.D. 500 to A.D. 950, the course of Christianity was downward. From the north successive waves of barbarian invaders, most of them pagans, poured into the Empire. Their inroads continued for more than five centuries. As each wave subsided, partial recovery and assimilation were followed by a fresh wave which destroyed still more of what had survived. From the southeast came the Arabs, bearing a new faith, Islam. They overran much of the eastern, all of the southern and part of the western shore of the Mediterranean. In these areas the Crescent slowly but in some places completely displaced the Cross. Ground was lost and the vitality of the Church ebbed.

Even in this long period of heartbreaking losses some gains were registered. Christianity was carried eastward until it was represented by small minorities across Asia into China. It moved southward into what is now the Anglo-Egyptian Sudan. More significantly from the standpoint of later history, it won many of the northern invaders and spread beyond the former borders of the Roman Empire into Germany, Scotland and Ireland. It not only tutored its barbarian converts in the rudiments of its faith but also became the vehicle of most of whatever of Greco-Roman civilization was transmitted to them.

Renewal

This period of decline, the most discouraging in the history of the faith, was followed by a major advance which was bounded roughly by the years A.D. 950 and A.D. 1350. The Scandinavians, the last of the barbarian invaders of western Europe, were baptized and the Cross was planted on Iceland and Greenland and probably carried by the converted Vikings to North America. The nucleus of the future Russian realm adopted the Christian name. After temporary disappearance from China, Christianity was once more represented in that Empire and was more widely disseminated in central Asia and south India than at any previous time. This extension was in part made possible by a fresh burst of life in the Church in western Europe which gave rise to new religious orders, among them the Franciscans and Dominicans. Moreover, in western Europe a civilization was emerging which was more profoundly molded in more of its aspects by Christianity than had been the civilization of Rome.

Great as were these accomplishments, in A.D. 1350 Christianity was not the faith of the most powerful peoples and the wealthiest cultures of the globe. Islam was found over about as broad an area and was the official religion of states more powerful than any in Europe. Buddhism was nearly as widely extended as Christianity and was potent among more numerous populations than any which bore the Christian name. Confucian China was larger and richer than all of western Europe. Christianity was now disseminated over more territory than any one religion had ever been, but in most of the areas which knew its name it was represented only by small minorities. The European states which called themselves Christian were collectively as well as singly on the periphery of civilized mankind. Through the Crusades and commercial and missionary enterprises of the twelfth, thirteenth and fourteenth centuries western European peoples had begun the expansion which was to come to flood in the great waves of exploration, conquest, migration, commerce and missions which began in the second half of the fifteenth century and continued into the twentieth century. As yet, however, western European peoples were a minor factor in the life of the globe.

Partial decline

Beginning not far from A.D. 1350 another recession of the Christian tide was seen. It was not so marked or so prolonged as its predecessor. Like the latter, it was characterized by loss of territory and decline in morale. The breakup of the Mongol Empire and the conquests of the Ottoman Turks were in large degree responsible for the territorial retreat. In Mongolia the Mongols became Buddhists and in central Asia and Russia they became Moslems. The Christian communities which had been scattered across Asia disappeared and on the continent of its origin Christianity became confined to minority enclaves from Persia westward and to the encysted Syrian Christians in India. The capital of Greek Christianity, Constantinople, fell to the Turks and its cathedral church was transformed into a mosque. The Crescent was pushed forward into the Balkans at the expense of the Cross. In western Europe, the remaining chief stronghold of Christianity, the majority church was divided by a distressing papal schism with rival pontiffs and then suffered from the leadership of the worldly Renaissance popes. Yet even in these unhappy years some advances were registered. The parts of the Iberian Peninsula which had remained under Moslem rulers were rewon by Catholic monarchs. The northern frontiers of Christianity were pressed forward in Russia and Lithuania. Within western Christianity there were signs of life, partly in movements deemed heretical by the official church and partly in schools of mysticism and such new groups as the Brethren of the Common Life.

Expansion

Soon after A.D. 1500 a new advance began which continued until about A.D. 1750 and carried Christianity over a greater area than it or any other religion had ever before covered. This territorial expansion was in part in consequence of awakenings within the Church. The advance was the more remarkable because of a striking cultural revolution. The civilization of Medieval Europe was passing. To the formation of this culture Christianity had made major contributions and the association had been intimate. Western Europe was now moving into a new age. Rising absolute monarchies sought, often successfully, to subordinate the Church to their respective administrations. Intellectual and aesthetic life was moving in a secular direction. The age of discoveries was carrying European power to other continents, notably to the Americas, and the conquests were accompanied by the ruthless exploitation of subject peoples. At the outset of the sixteenth century Christianity appeared to be dwindling, about to be ushered out as an anachronism. Again, however, as after the disintegration of the Roman Empire, Christianity displayed the ability to survive the death of a culture with which it had been intimately connected and, released from what had sometimes been embarrassing compromises brought by that association, broke out in fresh power and exerted greater influence than before. In the sixteenth century the renewed life took the form of the Protestant and Catholic Reformations. Protestantism brought fresh vigor to the faith in northwestern Europe and what is often termed the Counter-Reformation cleansed the Church of southern and much of central Europe of many of its worst abuses. The major colonizing powers were Spain and Portugal, Roman Catholic in allegiance. The chief territorial expansion was, therefore, by the Roman Catholic form of the faith. This spread was due in no small degree to a new order, the Society of Jesus, which had come out of the movement. Yet Protestantism also carried Christianity to new territories, mainly in North America, the West Indies, India and the East Indies. The Russians bore Eastern Orthodoxy across Siberia and, not long after 1750, into North America. By A.D. 1750 Christianity was found on all five continents and in all the major population groups of the globe, including India, China and Japan. It was more widely influential than ever before. It greatly mitigated the harshness of the impact of Occidental upon non-Occidental peoples. In the European settlements in America it was the main impulse responsible for education. In Europe it was potent. It stimulated the emergence of new types of education, it inspired great music, art and literature, it was the impelling motive in the origins of international law, and it gave rise to the first pure democracies.

Recession

The period which began not far from A.D. 1750 and which lasted until A.D. 1815 was more of a pause than a recession. The pause was due to a combination of factors. These included the decline of the chief missionary nations of the preceding century, Spain and Portugal, recurrent and prolonged persecutions in China and Japan, the suspension of the major Roman Catholic missionary agency, the Society of Jesus, a rationalistic trend in European thought and a series of wars and revolutions which shook Europe and the Americas and which culminated in the French Revolution and the Wars of Napoleon. Yet very little territory was lost. Moreover, within Protestantism revivals were beginning which were to usher that branch of the Christian movement into the greatest expansion in its history. Pietism on the continent of Europe, the Great Awakening in the Thirteen Colonies, the revivals which marked the turn of the century in the young United States and the Evangelical Awakening in the British Isles were the precursors of a phenomenal burst of life in nineteenth-century Protestantism.

"*The great century*"

Much in the nineteenth century was adverse to Christianity. In traditional Christendom, Europe and its colonies, several outstanding trends were inimical to the faith. Again a culture with which Christianity was interwoven was passing. The scientific movement appeared to be rendering Christianity intellectually untenable. The theory of evolution seemed to discredit the traditional Biblical account of creation. The application of historical methods to the Bible undermined the confidence of many in the inspiration of that book. More serious still, the scientific approach, with its reliance upon human initiative and reason, appeared to leave no room for the very heart of the Christian faith, Divine revelation. The absorption of millions in the pursuit of the comforts and the wealth made possible by the new machines distracted attention from religion. Great migrations, some of them to the new industrial and commercial centers and some overseas to the Americas, Australia and New Zealand, moved millions from their hereditary environment, including the Church, and from lands where the Church was supported by the state and by public taxation to lands where, if it were to be maintained, it must depend upon voluntary contributions.

In spite of these threats, the nineteenth century witnessed tremendous vigor in the Church. The new life was seen in the Roman Catholic Church. It was partly through that church that the expansion was achieved. As we suggested a few paragraphs above, more new orders and societies came into being within that church than in any previous hundred years. The control of Rome over the church was strengthened. More than ever before the Roman Catholic Church was a closely knit organization under the immediate direction of the pope. However, it was in Protestantism that the new life was chiefly seen. It was through Protestantism that the expansion of the faith was mainly accomplished. More than any period up to that time, the nineteenth century was the Protestant century. This fact, as we shall see, has immense significance for our day. The new life in Protestantism was displayed in great revivals, such as those associated with the names of Charles G. Finney and Dwight L. Moody, and with such movements as led to the formation of the Free Church of Scotland and to the Anglo-Catholic trend in the Church of England. It expressed itself in the rapid growth of the Sunday schools, in the rise of the Young Men's and Young Women's Christian Associations, in the emergence of the Young People's Societies of Christian Endeavor, and in the multiplication of Bible societies and of societies for home and foreign missions. Since the two nations which had the largest extension of territories, wealth and population, the United States and Great Britain, were predominantly Protestant, that branch of the faith shared in their prosperity and expansion. Protestantism grew and was planted in new regions proportionately much more rapidly than was Roman Catholicism or Eastern Orthodoxy.

The nineteenth century saw an unprecedented expansion of Christianity. Reinforced by the fresh surges of life within the Church and challenged by the opportunities afforded by the continued spread of the peoples and cultures with which it had become intimately associated, Christianity was carried over a larger proportion of the surface of the globe and to more peoples than had been true of it or any other religion or set of ideas. Ardent missionaries, lay and clerical, planted it securely among peoples of European stock along the frontiers of their settlement. This was seen in an astonishing manner in the United States, Canada, Australia, New Zealand and South Africa. To a lesser degree it was also witnessed in Latin America. By the year 1914 there were few non-Occidental peoples among whom Christianity was not a growing force. In some of these, notably the Indians of the United States and Canada, the Negroes of the United States and the Polynesians of the Pacific Islands, Christians were large minorities. In others, strikingly in the great population masses in India, China and Japan, they were numerically inconsiderable albeit growing minorities.

Moreover, in the nineteenth century Christianity attained to far greater influence in the entire human scene than at any previous time. This was seen partly in what euphemistically but with only a partial approach to accuracy was termed Christendom, the peoples among whom the faith had longest been represented and nominally accepted. Here it showed its power in stimulating education, as on the frontier in the United States, and in giving rise to movements to combat entrenched evils, such as Negro slavery, the excessive use of alcohol and the habit of war. It was the impelling force in the initial stages of the modern nursing profession. It was the propulsive motive in the pioneer efforts to provide more intelligent and humane treatment of the insane. It was prominent in the inception of prison reform.

In the non-Occidental portions of the world the increase in the influence of Christianity was especially marked. Because of Christianity more languages were reduced to writing than had been given that medium of expression in all the previous history of the race. Through it new systems of education were begun in such vast areas as China and Africa south of the Sahara. By it modern medical care was introduced to Negro Africa, and the beginnings were made of a new medical and nursing profession in China. In many lands Christian missionaries helped in famine relief, in bringing in new food plants and improved methods of agriculture, and in bettering the lot of women. The Church became the most widespread of all institutions.

5. THE PRESENT AGE

The events of August, 1914, ushered mankind into another new era. In the last three decades two world wars have swept the planet. Western civilization is once more clearly in revolution. In non-Occidental lands a double revolution is in progress. The impact of Western civilization is bringing the disintegration of the inherited cultures. Since that civilization is itself in process of kaleidoscopic change, non-European peoples are experiencing both the disruption of their familiar environments and the bewildering changes in the culture which is inducing that disruption.

Dangers

In consequence, Christianity has again been confronted by a now familiar crisis. An age and a culture from which it had been seemingly inseparable are passing. The question once more arises whether the faith can endure. Can it shape human culture to its mind? Can it even survive, a minority force? Certainly the threat is acute. In itself war is unfavorable to Christianity. Preoccupation with it, the sag in morals which inevitably accompanies it, and the vast shifts of population induced by it have militated against the faith. Some of the most striking and extensive of the revolutions have regarded it with hostile eye. This was notably the case in Russia and only to a slightly less degree in Germany. Some phases of the Chinese revolution and of nationalism in India have been anti-Christian. The trend toward bringing all aspects of life under the control of government, even when not overtly unfriendly, has limited some of the traditional functions of the Church, such as education, youth organizations and marriage, and has demanded exclusive allegiance to the State, even against the claims of God. The secularizing trends and the religious skepticism of the nineteenth century have gained in momentum.

In large parts of its historic strongholds, numerically Christianity has lost ground. This has been the case in such major lands as Russia, Germany and France. Even in Great Britain the percentage of communicants in the population and the church attendance have declined. In several areas in which Christianity had been the professed faith of the community it now holds the unflinching loyalty of only a minority. In some nations, such as Norway, Sweden, Denmark, Italy, Spain, Portugal and several of the countries in the Balkans and central Europe, a state church or churches have the support of government. In England and Scotland established ecclesiastical structures persist, although weakened by dissenting religious bodies and by outright indifference. Yet in Europe the drift has been away from such a connection and toward indifference or open repudiation. In the United States the percentage of church members is still growing and in such British dominions as Canada and New Zealand it shows no diminution. However, in the United States the increase in church membership has been paralleled by what appears to be a rising religious illiteracy. Obviously Christianity is in one of its most crucial stages.

Progress

Yet in the three decades since the year 1914, when viewed against the background of mankind as a whole, in four striking respects Christianity has made progress.

In the first place, Christianity has become more nearly evenly distributed over the face of the planet. While in Europe it has lost ground numerically, in most areas outside that continent it has gained in adherents both actually and in proportion to the total population. We have seen this in the United States. It is true of Protestantism in Latin America, notably in Brazil. In Africa south of the Sahara Christians have multiplied more than fivefold. In India, the East Indies, China and Japan they have more than doubled. In all of these lands they still constitute only a minority. Indeed, in 1946 they are only about 2 per cent of the population of India, about 1 per cent of that of China and about one half of 1 per cent of that of Japan. More than at any time since the first three centuries of its life, Christians are a self-conscious minority in an unfriendly world. Yet that minority is more widely and more nearly evenly distributed over the earth's surface than it has ever been. The majority of Christians is still in the Occident, but in Europe they are declining and in most of the non-Occidental world they are gaining.

In the second place, Christianity has become more deeply rooted among more peoples than at any previous time. This is seen in the emergence of indigenous leadership among non-European peoples and in the growth of self-government and self-support in the non-Occidental churches. Until the post-1914 years these churches had been so dependent upon the founding churches of the Occident that they seemed to be aspects of ecclesiastical imperialism. In the three decades since 1914 this situation has been rapidly altered. The transition is by no means completed, but it is in process of being accomplished. Roman Catholics have been greatly augmenting the numbers of indigenous priests and nuns in non-Occidental lands and have been consecrating scores of native bishops. Protestants have been multiplying their indigenous clergy and lay leadership and have been rapidly turning over to them the administration of the churches and of the educational, medical and other institutions founded by their missions. In the Roman Catholic Church fully autonomous national units are impossible. Yet within the structure of Roman obedience national organizations have been emerging. For the larger Protestant "younger churches" full ecclesiastical independence of the "older churches" is being achieved. Missionaries from the "older churches" are still needed and welcomed, but more and more they go as colleagues to serve under the indigenous leadership. The Church's rootage is no longer so predominantly in the Occident. For the first time Christianity is in fact as well as in aspiration becoming a world faith. Indeed, it is the only religion of which this can be said.

In the third place, Christians are being knit into a world-wide fellowship. Since the first century internal divisions have been characteristic of Christianity. These have by no means been fully overcome. Yet as never before progress is being made toward transcending them. It is particularly marked in Protestantism. This is the more remarkable in view of the fact that Protestantism has been the most fissiparous of all the main wings of Christianity. The trend toward unity is seen in several directions. Christians of many denominations join in such world-wide organizations as the Young Men's and Young

Women's Christian Associations and the World's Sunday School Association. The churches share in the International Missionary Council, the Universal Christian Council for Life and Work, the World Conference on Faith and Order and the World Council of Churches which has arisen out of the two former bodies and which in 1946, although still in process of formation, has been approved by more than ninety ecclesiastical bodies. The International Missionary Council is composed of delegates of regional bodies which in turn are made up of representatives of churches or of societies most of which are the official organs of churches. This ecumenical movement is predominantly Protestant (if the Anglicans be included in this designation), but in some of its aspects several of the Old Catholics and smaller Eastern churches are represented and in limited phases even a minority of Roman Catholics co-operate.

In the fourth place, in the post-1914 world Christianity has been more widely influential than ever before. This assertion seems to be contradicted by the facts. Have not these years seen the most extensive destruction ever wrought by war? Have not these decades spanned revolutions, especially in the traditional heart of Christendom, which have dealt body blows to the churches? Against these negative and disheartening conditions is the fact that in the non-Occidental portions of the globe Christianity is playing a larger part than it did on the eve of 1914. In China Sun Yat-sen, the man who has done more to mold his people than any other of the century, was a Christian. The outstanding leader of China at the present time, Chiang Kai-shek, is a Christian. In addition to these two, other, less prominent Christians have been having a part in shaping the new China. Through them the faith, while by no means dominant, is far more potent in Chinese life than it was thirty years ago. In India the mounting stirrings of life among the outcastes, with a striving, often blind, toward a less degrading existence, has been in large part from Christianity. The most powerful individual in post-1914 India has been Gandhi. Gandhi is a Hindu, not a Christian, but he has been profoundly impressed by Christ and through him Christ is more to be reckoned with in India than before the year 1914. In many other non-Occidental regions Christianity is clearly of growing importance. Non-Occidental mankind is considerably more than half of the human race.

Moreover, it is by no means proved that Christianity has declined in its effect upon the Occident. If numerically it has lost ground in Europe, in some areas the surviving minority has displayed augmented vigor. In two organizations of Occidental origin but of world-embracing scope, the League of Nations and its successor, the United Nations organization, Christianity has clearly been a formative factor. Even in some of the revolutions which are anti-Christian, Christianity has contributed to the basic ideology, notably Marxism—although its genius has been strangely distorted and perverted in the process. In these and other respects since 1914 the Christian minority has been exerting world-wide influence which has been appreciably greater than before 1914.

One phase of the effect of Christianity must be singled out for comment. This is partly because of its permeation of much of modern and particularly of Occidental life and partly because of its peculiar relation to the faith. We refer to the humanitarianism which has been so characteristic of the Occident for at least the past century and a half. It has displayed itself in a wide variety of ways. The movements against war, the tendency to regard colonial possessions as a trust for the peoples of those regions, the projects for bettering the lot of underprivileged elements in the population, the endeavors to make the modern city more wholesome for the dwelling of man —these and scores of similar efforts basically stem largely from Christianity. They are derived from a value placed upon man which is of Christian origin and their advocates are nerved and sustained by a faith in the possibility of achieving them which historically has its source chiefly in a belief in the God and Father of the Lord Jesus Christ and in a conviction of the dependable character of the universe which issues from that spring. Yet much of this humanitarianism is being progressively divorced from Christianity and is becoming associated with a variety of humanism which regards belief in God as outmoded. Among many of the intelligentsia nontheistic humanism is a kind of orthodoxy which scorns Christianity as obscurantist. If the divorce were ever fully accomplished it is probable that this humanitarianism would languish and eventually die. The hard realism of much of current communism, with its professed concern for human beings in masses but its ruthless treatment of individuals who are in its way and its inclination to depart from internationalism and to become a support of accentuated nationalism, may well be evidence of the direction in which such a humanitarianism would move. The Christian faith and the Church with its devotion to the cure of souls inspired by the conviction of the priceless worth of every individual as potentially one who may have eternal and growing fellowship with the God and Father of the Lord Jesus Christ, are essential to the continued pressing of the struggle for a social order in which each member will be valued and none exploited or liquidated.

6. THE OUTLOOK

How far does the past enable us to forecast the future? Are there long term trends which because of their strength and their growth give indication of persistence and increase? Prophecy is notoriously fallible. Yet certain generalizations can be ventured which appear to arise out of the facts.

The prominence of the United States

One is the increasing prominence of the churches of the United States in the world scene. The impoverishment of Europe and the British Isles in two world wars has speeded the shift of power to the United States and Russia. Of these two, the United States is the stronger. Moreover, in Russia the outlook for the Church is highly precarious while in the United States the Church appears not to be waning but waxing. The churches of the United States certainly are challenged as never before by the position which the nation holds.

Expansion and unity

In the second place, the tendency which has been so marked since the beginning of the sixteenth century toward the world-wide extension of the Christian faith is probably not to be abated. We cannot yet be sure of what the late war has done to the churches in some non-Occidental lands. We know that missionary staffs have been depleted and that the Continent of Europe and probably the British Isles cannot be looked to for as much financial support and personnel as in the recent past. Yet, if they will but use them, the churches of the United States possess the resources more than to make up the loss. Moreover, the "younger churches" have been so growing in numbers and leadership that we are probably to see the continuation of the movement toward the even distribution of the Christian forces the globe around.

A third trend which seems to be gaining momentum is that toward Christian unity. What organizational forms that unity is to take we cannot now fully know. Probably they will not be what is generally termed church union, the complete fusing of existing ecclesiastical bodies. We appear to be moving in the direction of a kind of unity in which there is great diversity. Presumably this diversity will be accentuated as the "younger churches" become larger and more independent of the founding bodies. They will be less Occidental. With that variety and the increasing contributions to the Ecumenical Church from other cultural traditions, Christianity will be less tied to the West. More and more it will be true of the Church that "they shall bring the glory and the honor of the nations into it."

Ascendant and varied Protestantism

Presumably, in the fourth place, the Protestant wing of Christianity will gain.

The Eastern churches, including those of Russia and the Balkans, suffer from a long adverse history and from the machinations of governments which are led by those who have disavowed all religion and who either are hostile to Christianity or aspire to use the churches as tools for political and imperialistic ends. Little or no leadership in the spread of the faith can be expected from them. The Roman Catholic Church is suffering severe blows which, in spite of its great strength, may reduce it to a declining force in the affairs of mankind. The historic center of the Roman Catholic Church is in Western Europe. Here is most of its leadership. From here have come by far the major part of the money and missionary staffs which have made possible its phenomenal world-wide extension. As we have suggested, western Europe has been dealt body blows and is rapidly receding from the proud dominance in wealth, culture and power which it has held for the past century. Presumably it is not to recover its former hegemony. This means a marked dwindling of the physical resources of the

Roman Catholic Church at its very heart and possibly an accompanying decline in spiritual vigor. The loss will be partly offset from the strong branch of the church in the United States and to a much lesser degree from a few other lands. However, the largest numerical body of Roman Catholics outside Europe, that in Latin America, appears to be sterile and moribund. It has not even provided all its own clergy and is sending very few missionaries to the Indians on its borders or to the enterprises of its church in other lands.

In contrast, the chief nineteenth- and twentieth-century strength of Protestantism has been in the British Isles, the British Dominions and the United States. Britain has suffered from the recent wars, but not so disastrously as most of western Europe. The Dominions have been much less affected. The United States has emerged from the wars the most powerful nation in the world. In all these nations Protestants (if Anglicans be included in that term) are in the substantial majority. In the next stage ahead, therefore, the advance of Christianity and the Universal Church is presumably to rest more with Protestantism than with any other wing of Christianity.

As a fifth point, we must note that the Protestantism which is to lead in this advance is to be somewhat different from the Protestantism of the past. It is to be a much more varied Christianity than has been heretofore known. At its outset, Protestantism was confined to a very small part of the earth's surface, northwestern Europe and the British Isles. It was primarily Teutonic in its adherents and, as its traditional names indicate, it was a protest and a reform, a conscious reaction against the prevailing Roman Catholic Christianity. It was divided and its main confessional (or denominational) expressions were segregated from one another—Lutherans in the north of Germany and in Scandinavia, Reformed in Switzerland, France, the

Netherlands and Scotland, and Anglicans in England. In the United States, which today contains the largest block of Protestantism, all varieties of that form of the faith are represented. They are forced by geography to rub shoulders and are interpenetrating one another. Here, too, the extreme wing of Protestantism is more potent than in any major European land. Baptists are numerically the strongest, followed by Methodists, with Congregationalists prominent, and with what have been state churches in Europe—Lutherans, Reformed, Presbyterians and Anglicans—with able leadership, but minorities, none of which has the privileged position enjoyed in the Old World. To these have been added characteristically American denominations, largely akin to the Baptists and Methodists. Protestantism has also spread to all the continents, to all the larger and most of the smaller nations, and to the vast majority of the tribes of the earth. Here, rather more than Roman Catholicism, it tends to reflect the color of its environment. Indeed, it would be in danger of so far conforming as to jeopardize the essence of the faith were it not for the ecumenical movement which knits together most of Protestantism in a world-wide fellowship. Moreover, Protestantism is changing because it is more flexible than is Roman Catholicism and therefore better able to adjust itself to meet the needs of the time. Traditional Protestantism has striking weaknesses. It tends to be individualistic, to divide endlessly, to stress the intellectual approach rather than the appeal to the total self and to be subjective, viewing the Church as for the individual rather than seeing the Church as a divine community which has a right to the allegiance of the Christian. Yet many of the leaders of Protestantism frankly face these weaknesses and seek to overcome them. For the period immediately ahead, Protestantism, modified, enlarged in its outlook and expanding, appears to be more and more the main stream of Christianity. The Eastern churches and the Roman Catholic Church will continue, but will be relatively less prominent.

The Church and the world

In concluding this paper, we must remind ourselves that a feature of the current scene which conditions all the rest is the mounting antagonism between Christianity and the world about it. When it has been true to its genius Christianity has always faced hostility. The disciples were warned by no less a person than their Lord: "Woe unto you when all men shall speak well of you." The New Testament insists that "in the world ye shall have tribulation." In some areas and periods the nominal acceptance of Christianity as the community faith has seemed to obscure antagonism. The secular atmosphere of our age and the rise of new aggressive ideologies which seek to control or displace the Church, together with the extensive defections in historic Christendom, have once more sharpened the lines of division. Always the Church is threatened by the penetration of the world into its fiber. That peril continues. It is especially acute where, as in the United States and Latin America, Christianity is still regarded as the religion of the community. Yet increasingly Christians are conscious of being a minority and are aware of the irreconcilability of their proper standards with those of the world about them. They must never remain content with being a minority. To rest complacently in that position or to assume the defensive is to become hereditary, encysted and sterile. If Christians are true to the genius of their faith they will always be striving to bring all men everywhere and all phases of life in subjection to Christ. They must recognize the paradox that the kingdom of God is never to come fully within history, yet that they must always have as the prayer which directs their effort: "thy will be done on earth as it is in heaven." They must always be looking with confidence for the appearance of the Lord and the ultimate triumph of God and of His Christ.

Further Reading

FOSTER, JOHN. *Then and Now*: The Historic Church and the Younger Churches. New York: Harper & Brothers, 1942.

LATOURETTE, KENNETH SCOTT. "A History of the Expansion of Christianity" series. (7 vols.) New York: Harper & Brothers, 1937-1945.

———. *Anno Domini*. New York: Harper & Brothers, 1940.

———. *The Unquenchable Light*. New York: Harper & Brothers, 1941.

McNEIL, JOHN T. *The Christian Hope for World Society*. Chicago: Willett, Clark & Company, 1937.

WEIGLE, LUTHER A. *American Idealism*. New Haven: Yale University Press, 1938.

5

THE RESPONSIBILITY OF THE CHURCH FOR SOCIETY

Richard Niebuhr

1. The urgency of the question. 2. The meaning of Christian responsibility: responsibility to *and* for, *the kinds of irresponsibility, the scope of responsibility, responsibility to God, universal responsibility. 3. Irresponsible religion: the worldly church, false prophecy and false priesthood, isolationism in the Church. 4. The Church as apostle, pastor and pioneer.*

1. THE URGENCY OF THE QUESTION

The question of the Church's responsibility for the society in or with which it lives has been important and difficult since the beginning of Christian history. Neither Jesus nor his disciples found an easy answer to it. The Master was greatly concerned for the lost sheep of the house of Israel and loved Jerusalem with moving devotion. Yet his striking lack of interest in conserving the institutions and the culture of his society enables modern Jewish scholars such as Rabbi Klausner to maintain with some persuasiveness that the guardians of Jewish society were justified in rejecting his leadership. This apparently paradoxical attitude of the gospels is restated in variant forms in the other New Testament documents and in the writings of the Christian fathers. It is mirrored in the dual and antithetical types of Christian organization—the so-called "churches" which undertake to organize and defend the nations and cultures in which they function, and the so-called "sects" which withdraw from the world of non-Christian society.

Though the problem is so rooted in the nature of both Church and secular society that it is always present, yet it has a peculiar urgency for the modern church which is confronted with unusual evidences of misery in the life of human communities and of weakness within itself. Christians live today in and with nations that are either dying or over which the threat of doom hangs like a heavy cloud. Some of them are miserable in abject physical poverty; some seem hopelessly divided within themselves; some are powerful and affluent beyond the imagination of past years but full of internal anxieties and badgered by fears. In a general atmosphere of spiritual confusion political decisions are made uncertainly and hesitatingly. Apprehension of disaster has taken the place of the hope of progress as the dominant mood and motive of action.

Looking upon these societies, Christians, individually and in the community of the Church, are moved to weep over them as Jeremiah and Jesus wept over Jerusalem. They feel impelled to seek the peace of the cities in which they dwell as Paul and Augustine sought the peace of Rome. Their sense of responsibility has many roots—the love of neighbor inculcated by centuries of teaching and example, the faith in a God whose nature it is to order and redeem no less than to create. But one highly important root of the sense of obligation is the Christians' recognition that they have done not a little to make the secular societies what they are. In this respect the modern church is in a wholly different position from that which the New Testament church or even the church of Augustine's time occupied. The Christian community of our time, whether or not formally united, is one of the great organizations and movements in civilization; it is one of the oldest human societies; it has been the teacher of most of the nations now in existence. It cannot compare itself with the small, weak company of the early centuries living in the midst of secular societies that had grown up independently of it. The American, Russian and British empires as well as the German and Italian, challenge the Church to a sense of responsibility, therefore, which the Roman Empire could never call forth. They were not suckled in their infancy by wolves but nursed and baptized by the Church; it instructed them in their youth and has been the companion of their maturity.

The poignancy and urgency of the present question about the Church's responsibility for society are due then as much to the Church's consideration of its own plight as to its sympathy with the tragic empires and threatened cities of our age. It is doubtful whether Christian communities have suffered more from bad conscience at any time since the sixteenth century than they do now. There have been times when the Church felt itself more seriously threatened from without than it does today, but it has not often questioned its own adequacy so much as it does now and a major cause of this self-questioning is its sense of responsibility for the ruined and threatened societies with which it is associated.

When these things are spoken of many voices offer many counsels. No single, clear, prophetic cry challenges the attention and consent of Christians in mass. Perhaps no such voice will be heard; not every time of crisis is blessed with the gift of an apostle or reformer. Christian people may need to find their way today, as in some past periods of confusion, by means of simple, democratic, equalitarian discussion and decision, relying on no dominant human leader but on the Spirit in the churches. However that may be, in anticipation or without hope of prophetic revival, the time requires of all Christian folk in all these associations profound and continuous thought on the great issues of human life. In particular they need to reflect upon their responsibility for the states, nations and cultures of mankind so that their social decisions may be made in the full light of understanding rather than under the guidance of ancient habit or of emotionally charged catchwords. The following reflections are offered as a contribution to that end. Beginning with a definition of the Christian idea of responsibility they proceed to examine the erroneous or heretical forms of church responsibility and conclude with an effort to understand the positive content of the Church's social obligation by considering its functions as apostle, pastor and pioneer of humanity.

2. THE MEANING OF CHRISTIAN RESPONSIBILITY

Responsibility to and for

To be responsible is to be able and required to give account *to* someone *for* something. The idea of responsibility, with the freedom and obligation it implies, has its place in the context of social relations. To be responsible is to be a self in the presence of other selves, to whom one is bound and to whom one is able to answer freely; responsibility includes stewardship or trusteeship over things that belong to the common life of the selves. The question about the one *to* whom account must be rendered is of equal importance with the question about the what *for* which one must answer. The responsibility of rulers in political society varies not only with the number of functions they exercise but also with the sovereign to whom they must account for their rulership. The doctrine of divine right makes kings responsible to God alone and exempts them from all obligation to answer to the people. An extreme type of democratic doctrine teaches that governors are responsible only to the people they govern or to the majority of such people. Most modern democracies rest on a profounder and less popular conception of responsibility, both rulers and people being regarded as accountable to some universal principle—God, Nature or Reason—as well as to one another. The difference between these two conceptions of democracy is very great. For the first kind, the will of the people is sovereign and makes anything right or wrong; the representatives of the people are bound to obey the popular desire. According to the second conception, there is a moral law to which the people themselves owe allegiance and which governors, legislatures and courts are bound to obey even in opposition to the popular will. Such a conception of responsibility is implicit in the Bill of Rights.

The kinds of irresponsibility

The double reference implied in the concept of responsibility is clarified by an examination of the nature of irresponsibility. A person may be irresponsible, of course, in the sense that he lacks the true qualifications of a self, but if he has freedom or the ability to answer he may be morally irresponsible in the sense that he refuses to give account to those to whom he owes an answer for common goods, or in the sense that he offers a false account for the things entrusted to him. The first sort of irresponsibility is the kind which appears in the "public-be-damned" attitude once explicitly adopted by some great corporations and still somewhat in vogue, as when great manufacturing or financial concerns resist the right of the public to be given an accounting for human and monetary values. The second sort of irresponsibility appears in the economic life in the criminal acts of defaulters who falsify accounts. Politically the first sort of irresponsibility is manifest in the claim of nations to sovereignty, that is, to their claim to be under obligation to no power beyond themselves or to be justified in doing anything that seems necessary to preserve national existence. The second type of irresponsibility in the political life may be found in wastage of natural resources and particularly in the political exploitation of human lives, in the name of some high ideal.

The scope of responsibility

It is clear from these examples and from reflection on ordinary experience that the "*to-whom*" and the "*for-what*" elements in responsibility are closely connected. What a man is responsible for depends in part at least on the being to whom he is accountable. If he must make answer to a nation he is required to consider more values than if he must answer only to the stockholders of a mercantile company. Some of the perennial conflicts between representatives of political and of economic institutions seem to be due to the fact that the former generally have future generations in mind, while the latter rarely have, whether they are labor leaders or businessmen. If a man responds to the demands of a universal God then the neighbors for whom he is responsible are not only the members of the nation to which he belongs but the members of the total society over which God presides. If one must give account to a God who tries the "heart and reins," then one must answer for invisible as well as for overt acts. Responsibility is a universal feature of the social life of men, but the content of responsibility varies with the nature of the society to which men understand themselves to belong. In the company of God and of immortal souls even family responsibility is greater and more inclusive than in the company of nations and of men who are regarded as purely temporal beings. When men know that they stand before an infinite judge and creator the content of their obligation becomes infinite; they are required to exercise moral freedom in all areas of existence; no part of conduct remains a matter of indifference or subject to pure necessity; nowhere can man act without the liberty and obligation of moral agency.

Responsibility to God

These reflections on the general nature of responsibility have partly defined the form of the Church's accountability. The Christian community must conceive its responsibility in terms of membership in the divine and universal society; it knows that it must give answer to the God who is Lord of heaven and earth for everything with which it deals. It is necessary, however, if the Church's peculiar sense of obligation is to be illuminated, to define the Being to whom it is answerable as *God-in-Christ* and *Christ-in-God.* Indeed the Church itself must be described in these terms as the community which responds to God-in-Christ and Christ-in-God. A society which does not acknowledge its obligation to render account to this God and this Christ may call itself church but it is difficult to attach specific meaning to the term. Without the sense of moral dependence upon or of obligation to Christ a society lacks the moral reality of the Church. It may be a religious association of some sort but it is no church in the historic sense of the word. In the New Testament the Church appears, first of all, as the company of those who answer the call of Jesus and then as the fellowship of those who await his return. In both instances the Church responds to more than a historical Jesus. The disciples answer him as one who has authority. He is a prophet and more than a prophet. He has words of eternal life. There is a universal and an everlasting, a powerful, inescapable content in what he says and does. When they respond to him and follow him they respond and follow an eternal reality in the temporal. In awaiting his return they anticipate the coming of no finite and passing being, but of one who represents the victory of life over death, of love over evil. Before his judgment seat they expect to be required to give account not for their treatment of the limited number of friends and neighbors of the finite Jesus, but of all the sick, imprisoned, hungry, thirsty men of the world—the neighbors, brothers and companions of an omnipresent being. It is to God-in-Christ, to the universal, absolute and unconditioned in the particular that the early church renders account. Moreover it feels its responsibility to God-in-Christ not only as an eschatological community hastening toward a final and inclusive judgment, but also as a spiritual society, aware of the presence of the living Spirit of Jesus Christ, which is the Spirit of God. At every moment the company of Christians as well as each Christian renders account to the present Lord who is in the midst of every two or three persons meeting in his name. Its responsibility is not merely a preparation to answer in the future for all its words and deeds, but a continuous opening of the whole book of life to the inspecting and correcting activity of the ever-present Spirit of God.

We must invert the formula now and note that the being to whom the Church responds is Christ-in-God as well as God-in-Christ. The Church looks not only to the absolute in the finite but to the redemptive principle in the absolute. God, it believes and confesses, is love; He is mercy; He so loved the world that He gave His best-loved for its redemption; it is His will that the wicked should not perish but turn from their ways and live. To be a Christian church is to be a community which is always aware of and always responding to the redemptive principle in the world, to Christ-in-God, to the Redeemer.

Universal responsibility

It becomes clear that the content of the Church's responsibility is largely determined by the nature of the one to whom it renders account. Since it is God-in-Christ whom it answers the content of its responsibility is universal. It is not a corporation with limited liability. All beings existent in the world are the creatures of this creator and the concern of this redeemer. The questions, "Who is my neighbor?" and "What is good?" need to be answered in a wholly inclusive way by a Church which lives in the presence of and in expectation of the coming in power of this Lord. All men and all societies, all the realms of being, belong to the neighborhood in which this community of Christians is required to perform its functions for the common welfare. Whatever is, is good in the world of this God-in-Christ. It may be perverted, sinful, broken; but it is not bad, for God-in-Christ has made it and maintains it. Such universal responsibility is incompatible with a spiritualism that limits the Church's concern to immaterial values, with a moralism that does not understand the value of the sinner and the sinful nation, with an individualism that makes mankind as a whole and its societies of less concern to God than single persons, and with any of those particularistic and polytheistic theories of value and responsibility which substitute for God-in-Christ some other deity as the source of valuable being. Moreover, since it is Christ-in-God to whom account must be rendered the content of responsibility is always mercy. The Church is not responsible for the judgment or destruction of any beings in the world of God, but for the conservation, reformation, redemption and transfiguration of whatever creatures its action touches. Whatever may be said in terms of the eschatological parable about the future role of the Church as judge of the nations, nothing belongs to its present responsibility for which it cannot answer to the one who gave his life as ransom and whose whole activity was a seeking and saving of the lost.

3. IRRESPONSIBLE RELIGION

From this general description of the Church's responsibility we must now move to the consideration of its accountability for society. The nature of the latter may be illuminated for us to some extent if we consider, first of all, the ways in which the Church has been and can be socially irresponsible. Two sorts of temptations seem especially prevalent in history, the temptation to worldliness and the one to isolationism. In the case of the former the "*to whom,*" in the case of the latter the "*for what,*" of responsibility is mistakenly defined.

The worldly church

The first sort of irresponsibility or perversion of Christian social responsibility results from the substitution of human society itself for God-in-Christ. Instead of, "What doth the Lord require?" the question in the mind of the church which has fallen into this temptation is, "What does the nation or the civilization require?" It thinks of itself as responsible to society for God rather than to God for society. In this situation the church is more concerned about social approval and disapproval than about the divine judgment, and its end is more the promotion of the glory of society than of God. The societies to which Christians may feel responsible are various. Now it is a nation, now the society of mankind as a whole; now it is the conservative, now the radical or revolutionary part of the cultural group in which the church lives. Social religion in distinction from religion that is loyal to God-in-Christ is readily identifiable when the human unit whose glory it seeks is a nation, as in the case of that section of the church in Germany which equated the Christian cause with that of National Socialism. It is not as readily identifiable when the unit whose glory is to be promoted is mankind as a whole. Bergson, for instance, in his excellent discussion of *The Two Sources of Morality and Religion* notes that defensive religion is connected with closed societies, such as nations, but in relating the religion of aspiration to the open society of mankind as a whole he does not apparently note sufficiently that mankind as a whole is also finite. From the point of view of Christian faith a humanistic church is closely akin to a nationalistic church. The substitution of any society for the infinite and absolute God involves the Church in a kind of irresponsibility in the course of which it actually betrays the society it seeks to serve.

What is true of the difference between responsibility to the smaller or larger human society is true also of the difference between the sense of accountability to the more conservative and to the more revolutionary elements in society. Generally social religion of the sort described which depends on public approval seeks the esteem of those parts of society which have been established in power and enjoy the prestige attached to customary authority. The worldly church is usually a church which seeks to maintain the old order in society and with it the power of the monarchs and aristocrats, of the owners of property and of other vested rights. However, the temptation to worldliness arises also when a radical or revolutionary group seeks to seize power and when a church undertakes to gain the approval of such a group. The former temptation is great because of the Church's interest in order, the latter because of its interest in the reformation of unjust order, but in either case if it seeks to gain the good will simply of society or parts of society and makes itself responsible to them for supplying certain religious values it has become irresponsible in a Christian sense since it has substituted men for God. This sort of worldliness is a protean thing. It appears as feudalist, capitalist and proletarian Christianity, as nationalism and internationalism, as the defensive faith of the educated classes or as that of the untutored.

False prophecy and false priesthood

The church which has fallen into this temptation seeks to supply the societies upon whose approval it depends with supernatural grace or with religious aid of one sort or another. It tries to render account to men for its stewardship of religious values. It is a mediator of God not in the true prophetic sense but in the fashion of the false prophets. It tends to give society the assurance that its form of organization and its customs are divinely ordained, that it enjoys the special protection and favor of God, that it is a chosen people. Many Thanksgiving Day proclamations and sermons offer clear-cut examples of such pious worldliness. Again the secularized social church may undertake to aid a human society in its pursuit of the great values of peace and prosperity. It may do this by endeavoring to persuade men that the order which is in effect has divine sanction, by threatening all protests against it with supernatural punishment, and by scores of other more or less creditable devices. In ancient times and by non-Christian folk the usual method for gaining divine approval was by way of sacrifice. In more sophisticated times social religion may try to serve society by subjective and psychologically effective means, seeking to supply not so much a supernatural as a natural, psychological aid. It may try to generate "moral dynamic" by means of worship, assuage the passions with the aid of prayer and stimulate "good will" by means of meditation. It may turn its educational work into an effort to create "good citizens" or effective revolutionaries. The line between a Christian conduct that is responsible to God and one which is responsible to society is often hard to discover in such situations, but whenever worship has become subjective, that is, directed toward effecting socially desired changes in the worshiper, and education has become moralistic, it seems safe to assume that one is dealing with worldly religion.

The temptation to this sort of irresponsibility is particularly great in the modern world. It is great because human societies, in the form of nations and of civilizations, have become very powerful and seem to hold in their hands both the blessings and the curses that are to be visited on men. The belief that the fate of mankind depends on the decisions of the leaders of empire is widespread and pervasive. The temptation is enhanced by the long nurtured illusion of social progress, which leads men to believe that the meaning of human existence must be realized in some organization of human societies dwelling on the planet. Again the tendency to look upon all matters from a social point of view has increased the temptation of the Church to consider itself as responsible to society. Much social science, including the sociology of religion, has tended to erect society itself into a kind of first principle, the source of all human movements and institutions. It has not only described the relations of religion to other functions in social life but seemed to explain it as nothing but a social function. When the Church has accepted this view of itself it has given evidence of its complete fall into worldliness, for now it has substituted civilization or society for God as author and end of its being.

Isolationism in the Church

The most important reason, doubtless, for the prevalence of such "social religion" in modern Christian churches is their reaction against the isolationism which long characterized many of them. Isolationism is the heresy opposite to worldliness. It appears when the Church seeks to respond to God but does so only for itself. The isolated church is keenly aware of the fact that it must answer to God-in-Christ for all its deeds and for all the values it administers. But it thinks of itself as the being for which it must answer and it regards the secular societies with which it lives as outside the divine concern. Its attitude toward them is like that of certain Israelites toward the Gentiles or of Greeks toward barbarians—they are beyond the pale. What is required of the Church, according to this conception, is the intense development of its own life and the careful guarding of its holiness. This holiness religion is intensely self-regarding both with respect to the individual Christian and with respect to the Christian community. It thinks of the secular societies as antagonists of the Christian Church and as beyond the possibility of redemption. They are not only mortal but sinful and must be shunned so far as possible because contact with them is defiling. The Church, on the other hand, is the community of those who are to be saved from sin as well as death. It is the ark of salvation and the concern of its officers and crew is to see that it rides safely through the storms which bring destruction to other groups and other men.

It is not unfair to call this holiness religion irresponsible, for it is so in the definite sense that it disclaims accountability for secular societies. It rejects not only nationalism but nationality, not only worldliness but the world. The politics and economics and sometimes the family life of human groups are regarded by the extremer advocates of holiness faith as too defiling for contact. Hence the isolated church disclaims all interest in these social functions and with the disclaimer tends to abandon the secular societies to their own devices.

The history of the Church contains many examples of more or less extreme isolationism. Second-century Christianity, as represented in the epistles of John, in the *Didaché* and other contemporary writings, tended to make the commandment not to love the world nor the things that are in the world into an injunction to separate the Christian community from the political and cultural societies of the time. It thought of the Church as a new society for the sake of which the world had been created and which was destined to govern the world. Again in the monastic movement the temptation to isolationism had to be combated ever and again by the great reformers who sought to make the monk a servant of mankind rather than a seeker after his own holiness. Protestant sects also have been tempted to pursue a sort of perfectionism that was highly self-regarding while another stream in Protestant religion has been so spiritualistic and individualistic that the concrete life of the secular societies has been actually ignored as beyond the scope of a spiritual church's responsibility.

These two sorts of irresponsibility, worldliness and isolationism, are evidently interdependent in so far as either extreme tends to call forth a reaction toward its antithesis. The general tendency of the Church in the twentieth century has been toward a conception of social responsibility which virtually made it an agent of secular society. Under the circumstances it is not impossible that a strong countermovement will arise and that Christians will seek forms of church life that are independent of secular society not only in source but also in purpose. The true measure of the Church's responsibility is not to be found, however, by attending to either extreme or by seeking for a compromise position between them but rather by attending to the two aspects of Christian responsibility in the right way. The relation to God and the relation to society must neither be confused with each other as is the case in social religion, nor separated from each other as is the case in Christian isolationism; they must be maintained in the unity of responsibility to God for the neighbor.

4. THE CHURCH AS APOSTLE, PASTOR AND PIONEER

The Church's responsibility to God for human societies doubtless varies with its own and the nations' changing positions, but it may be described in a general fashion by reference to the apostolic, the pastoral and the pioneering functions of the Christian community.

Apostolic responsibility

The Church is by nature and commandment an apostolic community which exists for the sake of announcing the Gospel to all nations and of making them disciples of Christ. The function of the Church as apostolic messenger to individuals is clear-cut, but emphasis upon it ought not to lead to the obscuring of its mission to social groups. The Gospel must be announced in different fashion when it is addressed to America or to Russia from the way in which it is proclaimed to individual Americans or Russians. Here again no absolute distinction can be made but it does seem important and imperative that the Church should discharge its apostolic responsibility by envisaging the needs of men in their societies as well as in their isolation before God. This seems the more urgent in our time because the unbelief, the fear and sin of man come to exhibition more dramatically in the public life than elsewhere. The phenomenon of nationalism is religious in character; so also is the worship of civilization which seems to pervade the democratic societies. On the one hand, the social groups appear to be idolatrous in a sense that few of the individuals in them are; on the other hand, the idolatry of the great groups seems to arise out of that despair of God and the meaning of life for which the Gospel supplies the cure. As the apostolic Church it is the function of the Christian community to proclaim to the great human societies, with all the persuasiveness and imagination at its disposal, with all the skill it has in becoming all things to all men, that the center and heart of all things, the first and last Being, is utter goodness, complete love. It is the function of the Church to convince not only men but mankind, that the goodness which appeared in history in the form of Jesus Christ was not defeated but rose triumphantly from death. Today these messages are preached to individuals but their relevance to nations and civilizations is not adequately illuminated. The Church has not yet in its apostolic character made the transition from an individualistic to a social period which historic movements require. When it does take its social responsibility seriously it all too often thinks of society as a physical and not a spiritual form of human existence and it tends, therefore, to confine its care of society to interest in the prosperity and peace of men in their communities.

It is a part of the apostle's duty to continue the prophetic function of preaching repentance. The good news about the glory of divine goodness is neither rightly proclaimed nor rightly heard if it is not combined with the bad news about the great justice which prevails in God's world. It is impossible for the Church in Germany to give assurance to the German nation that it is not the will of God that this sinful people should perish without at the same time assuring the nation that its transgressions must be recognized and condemned. So the apostolic Church in America cannot announce the mercy of God without pointing out how this nation transgresses the limits assigned to men when it defrauds the Negro and refuses to condemn itself for the indiscriminate manner in which it made war in its use of obliteration bombing, or deals with defeated nations in the spirit of retribution rather than of redemption.

It is not enough that the Church should discharge its apostolic function by speaking to governments. Its message is to the nations and societies, not to the officials. A truly apostolic Church may indeed address presidents, legislatures, kings and dictators as the prophets and Paul did of old; but like them it will be less inclined to deal with the mighty than with the great mass, with the community as it exists among the humble. How the Church is to carry out this apostolic task in our time is one of the most difficult problems it confronts. Its habits and customs, its forms of speech and its methods of proclamation come from a time when individuals rather than societies were in the center of attention. Responsibility to the living God requires in this case as in all others an awareness of the immediate moment and its needs, a willingness to reconstruct one's own habits in order that the neighbor's needs may be met, a readiness to depart from tradition in order that the great tradition of service may be followed.

The shepherd of the lost

The Church discharges its responsibility to God for society in carrying out its pastoral as well as its apostolic functions. It responds to Christ-in-God by being a shepherd of the sheep, a seeker of the lost, the friend of publicans and sinners, of the poor and brokenhearted. Because of its pastoral interest in individuals the Church has found itself forced to take an interest in political and economic measures or institutions. Many of the early leaders of the social gospel movement were pastors whose concern for individual slum dwellers, the poor, the prisoners and the sick led them to attack the social sources of human misery and to understand the corporate character of human sin. Genuine pastoral interest in individuals will always lead to such results. The Church cannot be responsible to God for men without becoming responsible for their societies. As the interdependence of men increases in industrial and technological civilization the responsibility for dealing with the great networks of interrelationship increases. If the individual sheep is to be protected the flock must be guarded.

The pastoral responsibility of the Church for society is, however, direct as well as indirect. Compassion and concern for the Jewish people as a whole, pastoral interest in the defeated nations and in the victors who stand in great moral danger characterize the Church which responds to the God who not only creates men but also their societies. This pastoral mission of the Church to the nations includes all those measures of large-scale relief and liberation which the times call for.

It cannot be sufficient for the Church to call upon the governments of nations to feed the hungry and clothe the naked. Direct action is required here as elsewhere.

The Church as social pioneer

Finally, the social responsibility of the Church needs to be described as that of the pioneer. The Church is that part of the human community which responds first to God-in-Christ and Christ-in-God. It is the sensitive and responsive part in every society and mankind as a whole. It is that group which hears the Word of God, which sees His judgments, which has the vision of the resurrection. In its relations with God it is the pioneer part of society that responds to God on behalf of the whole society, somewhat, we may say, as science is the pioneer in responding to pattern or rationality in experience and as artists are the pioneers in responding to beauty. This sort of social responsibility may be illustrated by reference to the Hebrew people and the prophetic remnant. The Israelites, as the major prophets ultimately came to see, had been chosen by God to lead all nations to Him. It was that part of the human race which pioneered in understanding the vanity of idol worship and in obeying the law of brother-love. Hence in it all nations were eventually to be blessed. The idea of representational responsibility is illustrated particularly by Jesus Christ. As has often been pointed out by theology, from New Testament times onward, he is the first-born of many brothers not only in resurrection but in rendering obedience to God. His obedience was a sort of pioneering and representative obedience; he obeyed on behalf of men, and so showed what men could do and drew forth a divine response in turn toward all the men he represented. He discerned the divine mercy and relied upon it as representing men and pioneering for them.

This thought of pioneering or representational responsibility has been somewhat obscured during the long centuries of individualist overemphasis. Its expression in the legal terms of traditional theology is strange and often meaningless to modern ears. Yet with our understanding of the way that life is involved with life, of the manner in which self and society are bound together, of the way in which small groups within a nation act for the whole, it seems that we must move toward a conception similar to the Hebraic and medieval one.

In this representational sense the Church is that part of human society, and that element in each particular society, which moves toward God, which as the priest acting for all men worships Him, which believes and trusts in Him on behalf of all, which is first to obey Him when it becomes aware of a new aspect of His will. Human society in all of its divisions and aspects does not believe. Its institutions are based on unbelief, on lack of confidence in the Lord of heaven and earth. But the Church has conceived faith in God and moves in the spirit of that trust as the hopeful and obedient part of society.

In ethics it is the first to repent for the sins of a society and it repents on behalf of all. When it becomes apparent that slavery is transgression of the divine commandment, then the Church repents of it, turns its back upon it, abolishes it within itself. It does this not as the holy community separate from the world but as the pioneer and representative. It repents for the sin of the whole society and leads in the social act of repentance. When the property institutions of society are subject to question because innocent suffering illuminates their antagonism to the will of God, then the Church undertakes to change its own use of these institutions and to lead society in their reformation. So also the Church becomes a pioneer and representative of society in the practice of equality before God, in the reformation of institutions of rulership, in the acceptance of mutual responsibility of individuals for one another.

In our time, with its dramatic revelations of the evils of nationalism, of racialism and of economic imperialism it is the evident responsibility of the Church to repudiate these attitudes within itself and to act as the pioneer of society in doing so. The apostolic proclamation of good and bad news to the colored races without a pioneering repudiation of racial discrimination in the Church contains a note of insincerity and unbelief. The prophetic denunciation of nationalism without a resolute rejection of nationalism in the Church is mostly rhetorical. As the representative and pioneer of mankind the Church meets its social responsibility when in its own thinking organization and action it functions as a world society, undivided by race, class and national interests.

This seems to be the highest form of social responsibility in the Church. It is the direct demonstration of love of God and neighbor rather than a repetition of the commandment to self and others. It is the radical demonstration of faith. Where this responsibility is being exercised there is no longer any question about the reality of the Church. In pioneering and representative action of response to God in Christ the invisible Church becomes visible and the deed of Christ is reduplicated.

Further Reading

Brunner, Emil. *The Divine Imperative.* New York: The Macmillan Company, 1937.

Ehrenstrom, Nils, and Others. *Christian Faith and Common Life.* London: George Allen & Unwin, Ltd. 1938.

Niebuhr, Reinhold. *The Children of Light and the Children of Darkness.* New York: Charles Scribner's Sons, 1944.

TEMPLE, WILLIAM. *Christianity and the Social Order*. New York: Penguin Books, Inc., 1942.

VISSER 'T HOOFT, W. A., and OLDHAM, J. H. *The Church and Its Function in Society*. Chicago: Willett, Clark & Company, 1937.

6

THE LIMITATIONS OF THE CHURCH[1]

John C. Bennett

Introduction. 1. Two permanent dilemmas: inclusiveness versus *exclusiveness, unity* versus *freedom. 2. Some contemporary obstacles. Loss of knowledge and conviction. Racial and class divisions in the Church. The limitations of leadership.*

This chapter is deliberately one-sided. The author has often written about the reasons for faith in the Church, from the conviction that in our own time the Church has been going through a reformation in many aspects of its life, but he was asked to act in this chapter as an *advocatus diaboli* in order to emphasize the real limitations and weaknesses in the contemporary church.[2] It is one of the grounds for faith in the Church that the present leadership of Protestantism is critical of the

[1] In view of the designedly critical nature of the present paper, the reader is referred for a positive treatment of the Church to "Forms of Ecumenical Christianity," by John C. Bennett, Ch. 3, Vol. IV of "The Interseminary Series."—Ed.

[2] For a treatment of the most pressing contemporary obstacles external to the Church, see Clarence T. Craig, ed., *The Challenge of Our Culture*, Vol. I, "The Interseminary Series."

Church as an institution. This was one of the chief notes in the discussions at the Oxford Conference. The Protestant churches do show signs of real repentance. It is significant that Dr. Visser 't Hooft who, as general secretary of the World Council of Churches, is a central figure in the institutional life of the Church should write a book under the title, which is an adaptation of Pascal's description of man, *The Wretchedness and the Greatness of the Church.* The wretchedness of the Church is the theme of this paper but it should not be read without acknowledgment of the greatness of the Church.

The Church that is discussed in this chapter consists of the empirical churches. But at no point should these be considered in abstraction from the true Church which is present in part within these visible and imperfect churches. The churches are what they are in virtue of the fact that they contain members of the universal fellowship of Christ's faithful disciples. The empirical churches are carriers not only of a Gospel by which they are constantly inspired and judged but also of a stream of life in which there has been a concentration of the activity of God's spirit.

There is one inherent weakness in the Church that underlies everything else that can be said on this subject—the fact that the Church is a community of human beings with their characteristic sins and failures. This inherent weakness that is common to all human institutions takes a special form in the Church because of its dual character as a human and a divine community. Here lies the most virulent temptation to which the Church is subjected. It is the temptation to confuse the human factors in its life with those that are divine. Even the claim that within the Church there has been a concentration of the work of the Spirit is very dangerous. It tempts the Church to complacency and self-righteousness. When the Church goes uncriticized in the light of the purposes of Christ and when power within it is concentrated and unchecked, its sins acquire a rankness all their own. The rigidity, intolerance and blind conservatism of the Church have made it seem at times a major obstacle to liberty and to the more humane aspirations of men. It is one of the saving things about the Church that it raises up within itself sectarian movements that rebel against the crust of ecclesiastical abuses which forms so easily, against the ways in which the representatives of the institution distort or hide both the demands and the promises of Christ.

1. TWO PERMANENT DILEMMAS

We can see many of the contemporary problems of the Church against the background of two permanent dilemmas which the Church has always had to confront. The first is the dilemma of inclusiveness which invites invasion of the Church by the world *versus* exclusiveness which involves the temptation to self-righteousness. The second is the dilemma of unity *versus* freedom which arises out of the religious and intellectual limitations that make it impossible for Christians to see truth in the same light. To these dilemmas can be applied Reinhold Niebuhr's principle that there are no ultimate solutions in history, that our life must move from one proximate solution to another. The reason that each of these problems is intrinsic to the nature of the Church is that any solution will tend to give too great emphasis to one of two contrasting values and it will intensify the temptations which go with the exaggeration of that value. This is not a pessimistic conclusion. Proximate solutions may represent great advances if it is recognized that they are not ultimate.

Inclusiveness versus *exclusiveness*

How inclusive should the Church be in its membership?[3] How far should it accommodate itself to the institutions of the world? If it makes its standards of membership lax as is now the case in both Catholicism and Protestantism, even in American denominations which have a sectarian origin (see Baptist statistics!), it will inevitably become in large measure secularized. The history of American Christianity has been a history of exclusive sects becoming inclusive churches after the second or third generation. The conduct of their members becomes little different from that of ordinarily decent citizens outside the Church. The Church under these conditions may perform valuable priestly and pastoral functions. It may help to keep up the general community standard. It may preserve contact with the total community and with its major institutions including the state and in so doing may have considerable Christian influence. If there is freedom within it and if not too complete a bargain has been made with the world, it may hold before its members and before society at large without great distortions the Gospel which it represents. This will have its own effect, sometimes in spite of the Church itself. There is objectivity in the Gospel and it cannot be entirely obscured by its representatives. If the Church is primarily sacramental there is another kind of objectivity that although easily abused and ineffective as a moral corrective enables multitudes of souls to bear the burden of life and death. If there is some

[3] The first dilemma has been made familiar in one form in the contrast between the ideas of the church and of the sect in the sense in which Troeltsch used those words. Troeltsch has given these two words technical meanings that are important for most contemporary discussion of the Church. See especially his *The Social Teachings of the Christian Churches* (New York: The Macmillan Company, 1931), pp. 331-343.

approach to a sound combination of these two kinds of ministry, the result may have great positive value even though the Church has paid a high price in its accommodation to the world, and the Church itself may be changed at any time by its Gospel.

It is a weakness for the Church to become as much like the world as the Churches to which most of us belong. But when we try to correct that weakness and make the Church more exclusive we may do what at a given time is required but we run into weaknesses of an opposite kind. The first effect is divisiveness and the tendency to split into smaller and purer sects. But there are three other effects. There is an inevitable tendency toward self-righteousness in the Church. For a time this may be the price of heightened religious devotion and moral zeal, but the second generation of self-righteous exclusiveness may be without compensation. It may become a Church without love, a Church which is the reflection of the complacency and even of meanness among its members. A second result is the loss of contact with the community at large and, with that, the loss of many opportunities to save souls and to influence the character of institutions. A third result is that the exclusive church (sect) is so cut off from the main body of Christians that it loses the chance to be corrected or enriched by the larger fellowship.

Unity versus *Freedom*

The second major dilemma is the inevitable consequence of the fact that the human spirit sees truth from a limited perspective and so mixes truth with error. The divergencies between equally competent and equally sincere minds is a constant problem in the Church as it is in many other spheres. There are other reasons for the disunity of the Church than these differences of conviction, and they are found so tangled with such differences that it is hard to determine how important the latter really are. All that is claimed here is that these differences are not only a façade for other factors but that they do have their own effects. Many differences can be included within a united Church and others within a looser type of federation, but there remain differences which for as long a time as we can now foresee will continue to produce separation and conflict.

The chief of these differences is, of course, that which divides the Roman Church from the other churches of Christendom. Here we have to do not only with theological conflicts that might be comprehended within an inclusive Church but absolute jurisdictional claims countered by the absolute rejection of them. It is a very grievous thing that the Christian Church is divided in this way, both for itself and for its impact upon civilization. We Protestants speak hopefully of what the Church is doing but the Church to most of Europe and Latin America means the Roman Church. While that church is in a minority in this country its impact upon American urban life and upon policies of government has become almost as strong as that of Protestantism as a whole. The separation between Catholicism and Protestantism in America and the fact that they are in many ways working against each other without either Christian fellowship or mutual trust are very dark shadows upon the Church here. It is nothing less than appalling that, while we make great claims for the Christian Church, we must admit actual distrust of the one church that has most power in the world.

Roman Catholicism is not the only type of Catholicism and there are some difficulties in the relations between American Protestantism and the Anglo-Catholic wing of the Protestant

Episcopal Church or the Eastern Orthodox churches. But here fellowship and co-operation are possible in spite of real barriers. The Anglo-Catholics are themselves part of a remarkably inclusive church. Moreover, they represent a tendency that is present in many degrees and this helps to preserve continuity between them and Protestants. The Eastern Orthodox are now represented in the Federal Council of Churches and it is hoped they will soon be fully represented in the World Council of Churches. When questions of organic union involving intercommunion or mutual recognition of ministries are raised there are formidable differences between Protestants and these Catholics, but such differences are not incompatible with the sense of belonging to the same Christian community.

One other important religious difference is the contrast between forms of Christianity that have been influenced by modern criticism and those which represent a Confessionalism or a Biblicism that tries to be self-sufficient and resists intellectual criticism. In this case we may be dealing with differences which will pass, for many religious movements in America have begun with a similar intransigence and yet have gradually allowed themselves to be influenced by the central intellectual trends in American Protestantism. At the present time there is a converging of aggressively fundamentalist forces. They have gained considerable power in one major denomination and they are greatly strengthened by the popularity of the new sects. Indeed the casual radio listener would judge them to be an extremely important part of American Protestantism.

These differences which have real religious and intellectual roots help us to see the difficulty of giving sufficient emphasis to both freedom and unity. In the name of freedom we divide the Church into fragments. In the name of unity we may quench the spirit. In the name of freedom we may encourage people to miss the richness of the total Christian fellowship and of the full range of Christian truth. In the name of unity we may encourage the tolerance of indifference and cut the nerve of sincere conviction.

It is not only on theological issues that we find intellectual conflict that threatens the unity of the Church. Another area of profound differences is the convictions of Christians about social questions. Once the American churches divided over the question of slavery. Doubtless there were many other factors in these divisions as there were in the Civil War that followed them, but the controversy over slavery aroused such strong emotions that it proved impossible to solve other problems that in themselves would not have split the churches. In our time the attitude of the churches toward war has proved to be an ethical issue concerning which the Church as a Church has been able to give very little guidance because of the conflict of convictions within it, but the fellowship of the Church has not been broken by this conflict. There is a danger that where unity is maintained, as in this case, the two sides to the controversy may neutralize each other and leave the average churchman and the nation confused.

This is the best place to call attention to the results of disunity whether it be traced to real differences of conviction or to other causes. The break in fellowship between those branches of the Church which are as different in theology or piety as Catholics and Protestants or Missouri Lutherans and Congregationalists is clear enough and in itself a great evil. But even among those churches which represent the same general type of Christianity there is a great handicap in denominationalism. This is most serious in the local community where competitive churches often strangle one another though little more than the momentum of institutions keeps them apart. There is no entirely satisfactory method of establishing a new church in a new community because of this denominationalism. A community church is cut off from the influence of the larger Church and is in danger of succumbing to localism. A church of one denomination may not draw people of many backgrounds though there is a great deal of flexibility in denominational allegiance in American communities. A federated church which keeps the local church relation to two or more denominations probably provides the best method, but it is complicated and the younger generation has difficulty in feeling a part of the larger Church.

There are many evidences of the strength of the denominational spirit in spite of much effective ecumenical work. The most vital concrete activity in the churches seems to be proceeding on a denominational basis. The approach of the churches to students is an example of this. In recent years the more ecumenical type of student work has suffered in contrast to the vigorous denominational student movements. How can students be made conscious of the Church without having the denominational church emphasized? So far no very effective method is in sight. Several of the strongest and most progressive denominations are becoming more self-sufficient and more aggressive as denominations, not because their leaders lack a broad vision of the larger Church, but because they can work most effectively when they use their own denominational machinery.

2. SOME CONTEMPORARY OBSTACLES

We shall now turn to some contemporary obstacles of great importance for the churches in America. Each of them will reveal the pervasiveness of the dilemmas that have been discussed. There are many other obstacles that might be mentioned but three have been chosen for emphasis because they seem to the writer to have the greatest importance.

The widespread loss of knowledge and conviction concerning Christian truth

The first of these contemporary obstacles is the lack of distinctive Christian conviction and even of knowledge concerning the content of the Christian faith within the Church itself. This is not a surprising weakness in an inclusive Church, but in the modern period the inroads of secular assumptions have been so great in the Church itself that we find this to be our special problem. It is astonishing that three things can be true at the same time in America—a steady increase in membership in the Church, greatly improved opportunities for general education, a noticeable growth in religious illiteracy. Professor Latourette says in his account of contemporary American Christianity: "There were indications that the increasing proportion of church membership was paralleled by a growing illiteracy among a majority of those owning to this connection."[4] Put beside that sentence another which to some extent corrects it: "Yet by 1945 there were indications that for a growing minority the Christian faith was more intelligently held and given a more thoroughgoing commitment than had been true two decades earlier."[5] Who can explain the fact that while in 1890 the total number of Church members constituted 22.5 per cent of the population, after all of the "acids of modernity" have done their work the total number of members in 1944 was 52.5 per cent of the population?[6] These figures

[4] *Advance Through Storm*, Vol. VII, "A History of the Expansion of Christianity" series (New York: Harper & Brothers, 1945), p. 125.

[5] *Ibid.*

[6] *Year Book of American Churches*, 1945, (New York: Federal Council of the Churches of Christ in America), p. 151.

are a sign of the Church's opportunity but taken in connection with the growing evidences of religious illiteracy they also suggest the Church's failure to educate its own growing constituency.

The degree of the failure and the reasons for it may be debated by partisans of the various educational approaches but most of them would admit that all approaches have in large measure failed. The conventional Sunday school, the modern methods of religious education, the sermon as a medium for teaching, evangelism, have all left a disappointingly small deposit of knowledge and conviction. The Protestant churches have also failed to counteract the secularizing tendencies in public education, and they have not done much better in institutions of higher education of their own founding. Much of this is the result of our religious pluralism, not so much Protestant sectarianism as the necessity of doing justice to Protestants, Catholics and Jews in the same community. The fact that a private institution such as Harvard can propose a new program of liberal education and deliberately refuse to give religion any place in it is evidence enough that our problem has little to do at bottom with the separation of Church and State. More important is the separation of Christianity and culture.[7] It is difficult to believe that real awareness of the issues and a willingness on the part of Protestants to pay a high price for Christian influences in education might not have produced far better results. Whoever may be at fault, the churches are left today in a condition of great inner weakness because the Christian faith has so small a hold upon their members. Both education and evangelism will be needed to correct this and a change that is pervasive may have to wait upon a spirit-

[7] *General Education in a Free Society* (Cambridge: Harvard University Press, 1945), p. 39.

ual revival that churches cannot plan. At present it is difficult to discover much beyond confusion of counsel and there are few signs of any such revival. Yet it is not impossible that in 1950 we shall discover that the proportion of church members has continued to increase!

Professor Robert Hastings Nichols has shown how several factors peculiar to American life have produced a characteristically American conception of the Church which has resulted in a marked degree of secularization of the Church.[8] It is interesting to note that the very sectarian type of Christianity that has been dominant in American Protestantism and which in other contexts is a protest against the secularization of the Church has helped to make the Church more secular. The idea of the Church as a voluntary association of converted Christians, the stress upon the local church, the large place given to laymen, the acceptance of the principle of majority rule in the organizations of the Church, the fact of geographical isolation from the older churches of Christendom—all of these factors have tended to make the Church a reflection of the American community. Many of these things are good in themselves—individual conversion and lay initiative, for example—but the combination of them has made it difficult for the Church to resist the secularizing forces in American culture. In recent years there have been important corrective tendencies involving both the recovery of a distinctively Christian message on the part of many churchmen and the knitting together of many Christians into the fellowship of the ecumenical Church.

[8] See article, "The Influence of the American Environment on the Conception of the Church in American Protestantism," in *Church History*, September, 1942.

The reflection of racial and class divisions in the Church

The second contemporary obstacle is the way in which the Church reflects conflicts and divisions in the world. This is at the root of most of its ethical impotence. In our time the conflicts between nations have divided the Church less deeply than has been true at any time since the rise of modern nationalism. Among the communions that adhere to the World Council of Churches there has been a very notable gain at this point. But the struggles between the Roman Church and the Orthodox churches in eastern Europe, which are in part the reflection of conflicts among nationalities, are intensely bitter. There is also a considerable gulf between the Greek-speaking and Slavic-speaking Orthodox churches. The way in which the Soviet government is using the Russian Church to support its political policies in the Balkans is one of the most flagrant examples of the invasion of the Church by the world. To point to it as such should not be a signal for self-righteous criticism from churches which have been used in the past in similar ways, but it is very disturbing. In general it can be said that the Church has been surprisingly successful in bridging the chasms between enemies in the recent war but that there are few indications that it will be able to do much to bridge the chasm between Russia and the West which is now our greatest threat to peace. The conflict between Roman Catholicism and communism and the older conflict between Roman Catholicism and the Orthodox churches are calculated to make this chasm wider. The role of Protestantism here remains uncertain.

It is when we come to the racial and social divisions that are reflected in the Church that we encounter one of the greatest failures of the American Church. Professor Richard Niebuhr in *The Social Sources of Denominationalism* has shown how far the denominational divisions in American Protestantism correspond to social divisions in the nation. This book is one of the most indispensable books for all who seek to make the churches in America more effective instruments of God's purpose of reconciliation. Professor Niebuhr summarizes his criticism of our denominationalism in these words:

> It [denominationalism] represents the accommodation of Christianity to the caste-system of human society. It carries over into the organization of the Christian system of human society. It carries over into the organization of the Christian principle of brotherhood the prides and prejudices, the privilege and prestige, as well as the humiliations and abasements, the injustices and inequalities of that specious order of high and low wherein men find the satisfaction of their craving for vainglory. The division of the churches closely follows the divisions of men into the castes of national, racial, and economic groups. It draws the color line in the church of God; it fosters the misunderstandings, the self-exaltations, the hatreds of jingoistic nationalism by continuing in the body of Christ the spurious differences of provincial loyalties; it seats the rich and poor apart at the table of the Lord, where the fortunate may enjoy the bounty they have provided while others feed upon the crusts their poverty affords.[9]

American churches are racial churches. This is true of local churches almost universally. Denominations make a place for Negro and white Christians but there is often ecclesiastical segregation as in the case of the "Central" jurisdiction in the Methodist Church. There seems to be no solution in sight of the problem of the local church in a racially mixed community.

[9] Richard Niebuhr, *The Social Sources of Denominationalism* (New York: Henry Holt and Company, Inc., 1929), p. 6.

The usual pattern has been for the white church to preserve its identity as long as possible and then move or die, giving place to the Negroes who move into the neighborhood. The churches in their teaching are becoming more and more drastic in their criticism of racial discrimination and segregation. What they do on a national scale has promise. But on the local level both the policies and the attitudes of churches contradict their teaching and it is doubtful if those who are aware of this fact know what to do about it.[10]

The reflection of class differences in the Church is not quite so clear but it is still pervasive. The statistical picture is confused. Dr. H. Paul Douglass[11] denies that Protestantism as a whole is one-sided as a class institution but he admits that one factor in his calculations is the strength of Protestantism among Negroes. So, the statistics which on the surface suggest social inclusiveness in American Protestantism really point to the fact of racial segregation. The Federal Council of Churches is initiating a statistical study of this problem that should give more adequate guidance than we have at present. In the meantime, there are a few massive facts that are not in dispute. Local churches tend to be one-sided in their constituencies. Denominations are also one-sided whatever may be the total picture in Protestantism. The lay leadership in the

[10] A recent study made for the Federal Council of Churches shows that at least 90 per cent of the Negro Protestant church members are in separate denominations. A questionnaire sent to the churches of five denominations disclosed that there were at least 294 predominantly white churches in which Negroes participate. Usually these are churches in small communities where only a few Negroes live. In the transition area of a city with a large Negro population, the survey failed to discover a single "white" church which has Negro members.

[11] H. Paul Douglass and Edmund de S. Brunner, *The Protestant Church as a Social Institution* (New York: Harper & Brothers, 1935), pp. 51-52.

most influential Protestant denominations, with few exceptions, belongs to the middle-class world. The Federal Council Committee on the State of the Church in 1936 reported that "the leaders of the local Protestant churches, particularly those which have largest influence, do not belong to the stratum of the American people whose incomes are below $2000 a year." "And," the Committee added, "they are likely to look with hesitation and fear upon the struggle of the masses for better conditions of life." Some of the reasons for the social one-sidedness of Protestantism involve problems that seem insoluble. Catholics and Jews are much more numerous than Protestants in our industrial cities. Protestant worship is culturally divisive and it is difficult to see how it can be otherwise when the emphasis is upon preaching. The consequences of this cultural divisiveness are seen in the contrast between the newer sects and the older established denominations. So far as local churches are concerned, the way in which residential areas are divided often makes social inclusiveness difficult. Experiments with inclusive local churches are desirable but even more urgent is the effort to make the larger units of Protestantism, the denominations, socially inclusive.

Professor E. G. Homrighausen calls attention[12] to a recent study made by the Public Opinion Research Office of Princeton University of the income groups represented in the constituencies of the various denominations. The results based upon ten thousand cases selected "from various sections of the United States except the deep South" show the extent to which three income levels are represented in the denominations in the following table:

[12] *Theology Today*, January, 1946, p. 543.

	UPPER	MIDDLE	LOWER
Episcopalians	32%	35%	33%
Presbyterians	26	40	34
Congregationalists	20	39	41
Lutherans	10	43	47
Methodists	13	42	45
Baptists	9	27	64
Roman Catholics	8	28	64
Non-members	11	28	61
Total Population	16.6	35	48.4

These statistics confirm the contention of Dr. Douglass that Protestantism as a whole does represent all sections of the population. It is denominations that are one-sided. It should also be remembered that if one were to examine the group in the lowest income bracket in some denominations, the Congregational for example, a large percentage of the people would prove to be rural. That means that they would probably be highly critical of the urban workers. So far as social conflict is concerned the weakness of Protestantism among the industrial workers makes the religious divisions more serious than these figures suggest.

This division of the Church according to the social lines that divide men means that the life of the Christian community is itself a denial of Christian fellowship. This would be reason enough for condemning it. There are two consequences of this social stratification within the Church to which I shall call special attention.

One of them is that we often find that two kinds of religion develop within churches that draw their members from different social strata and that each of these two kinds of religion is a perversion of Christianity. Professor Liston Pope in his book, *Millhands and Preachers*, describes the types of religion that he found in the "mill churches" and the "uptown churches" in the North Carolina county that he studied. He says: "If religion in the mill villages is largely an escape from economic conditions, religion in the uptown churches is to a considerable degree a sanction of prevailing economic arrangements."[13] The authors of *Middletown*, an account of a more typical American community than those studied by Professor Pope, came to the same conclusion. The churches of the middle classes did nothing to disturb the complacency of their members. The churches of the poor were otherworldly in their emphasis and gave their members no understanding of the reasons for their poverty. In both cases we see one-sided forms of Christianity used as dope, in the one case to soothe the consciences of the comfortable and in the other case to call the attention of the poorer classes away from their condition in this world. In neither case was this done deliberately. It is possible for those who want no change in the economic order to use religion in this way, to pay the expenses of churches that fit their schemes and to refuse to support any minister who comes with a better understanding of the Gospel. On the other hand, the cynics who may take advantage of the weaknesses of religious leadership cannot expect to get very far for long unless that leadership is consciously sincere.

Another consequence of this kind of division in the Church is that it keeps the Church from being a solvent in the conflicts between classes and races. One could expect that if it were normal for conflicting groups to worship together, to stand together in a common confession of sin before God, some of the sting might be drawn from their conflict. In addition to the fact that this indirect result of common worship is lacking,

[13] Liston Pope, *Millhands and Preachers* (New Haven: Yale University Press, 1942), p. 92.

there is also lacking the possibility of mutual correction of judgment about controversial issues within the same church. These issues are seldom a matter of black and white. There is something to be said on both sides of most controversies and the process of reaching a Christian consensus on any such question depends on the participation of those whose interests and experiences differ. The lack of this kind of mutual correction puts a very difficult burden on the minister who is aware of his social responsibilities. It becomes necessary for him to represent the valid elements in the interests of those who are not present in his congregation. This sometimes puts him in the position of opposing his own laymen on issues concerning which they feel deeply. How much better it would be for the church if there were among the laymen an adequate representation of both parties to the controversy. Both parties to the controversy need to be kept at the same time under Christian criticism.

The limitations of leadership

A third contemporary obstacle is the very widespread spiritual and intellectual mediocrity in the leadership of the Church. Here we shall limit ourselves to the situation within American Protestantism. The reader should be reminded of the deliberate one-sidedness of this chapter, for the writer has no intention of making sweeping generalizations (certainly none that necessarily includes the reader!). It may be true that on the average in religious devotion, moral integrity or professional competence, the Protestant ministers in America at the present time compare favorably with large bodies of clergy in any period. Certainly there have been periods in which the conditions among the clergy have been far worse! Also, men under testing are often better than they seem in quiet times. One hears that chaplains were at their best near the front lines. Almost all of the clergy of Norway showed that they had heroic stature, to mention only one country where the church situation was very clear under the German occupation. I wonder if before the test came they seemed any better than the average among us. Perhaps they were no better before the test came than the one thousand Danish clergymen whom Kierkegaard dismissed as one thousand professionals who did little more than make a living out of the Cross of Christ![14]

The local Protestant church is too dependent for the quality of its life upon the personality and gifts of its ministers. In most denominations there is no part of the service of worship which the minister cannot turn into an offense. A thoughtful chaplain visited several churches recently in Minnesota, Wisconsin, Illinois and Texas, and he wrote to me: "I came to pray and remained to scoff." He described one of the services as follows: "On the floor stood the Communion Table, a profusion of summer flowers hid the cross and dining table candle sticks. . . . Above the cross loomed the big pulpit with the little preacher. The man is above the table of the sacrament. He towers above the cross. Man is central."

He may have been hypercritical but much of the time man is central and if the man in question is not a helpful mediator of the Gospel almost all may be lost in that situation. Great gifts are not necessary—but at least the right kind of religious awareness and the right kind of humility that will keep the minister from calling attention chiefly to himself. In the Bible and in liturgies that may be used quite freely there is the possibility of the minister's pointing beyond himself to God, to Christ, to the Gospel, to the larger Church. Where the min-

[14] *Attack upon "Christendom," passim.*

ister does that, though the sermon be poor, all is not lost for the worshiper. I think that it is a safe generalization that the greatest single weakness of American Protestantism is to be found in the number of local churches in which the worshiper is frustrated. (One should add to these the number of local churches where the worshiper would be frustrated if he understood more fully than he does the meaning of the Gospel.)

We are very close here to an intrinsic limitation of the Church closely related to the first one discussed. If it emphasizes the importance of the personal sincerity and depth of the individual minister it makes worship very precarious for the worshiper, too much dependent on an accidental factor. If it separates worship from the personality of the priest as Catholicism does in theory, it encourages a religiously unreal and an ethically indifferent sacramentalism. Both Protestantism and Catholicism have an unsolved problem here.

The weakness of the leadership in American Protestantism can be seen in other ways. One kind of evidence of this weakness is the proportion of inadequately trained ministers. In the study of theological education completed in 1935 it was discovered that at that time in nineteen white denominations 50.4 per cent of the churches were served by ministers who had had neither a college nor a seminary training and that only 20.3 per cent were served by ministers with both college and seminary training.[15] All that can be done to increase the number of trained ministers will be important and it is encouraging that the major denominations are continually raising their standards. But our real problems lie deeper than this. I ask the reader to consider each of the other limitations of American

[15] Mark A. May, and others, *The Education of American Ministers,* Vol. II (New York: Institute of Social and Religious Research, 1935), p. 14.

churches discussed in this chapter and ask himself how far the denominations that have a high proportion of trained ministers have escaped any of them. Even my generalizations about the weaknesses of leadership come from observation of those denominations that place great emphasis upon both college and seminary training.

We may see this weakness in the conceptions of the Gospel that underlie preaching in thousands of churches. This preaching may have the faults of a narrow fundamentalism, or it may do no more than soothe the complacent and evade every disturbing moral problem, or it may be the kind of moralistic exhortations that leave unhealed those whose consciences are already awakened. Or it may be a jumble of unrelated platitudes and anecdotes. The writer distrusts his own generalizations about the content of preaching, but recently a board secretary in whom he has much confidence said that he becomes more pessimistic about the Church the more he analyzes the sermons that he hears. He said that they usually had one of two faults—"dry rot" or an irrelevant idealism.

We may see the weakness of Protestant leadership in the fact that it is very widely reported by those who work among ministers that a large proportion of them have a defeated attitude and want to move more than anything else. Many of them should move and I am not criticizing them, but there is a vast waste in some of the denominations that grows out of the fact that men lose heart and churches run down because it is so difficult to move a man to the right church or to deliver any church from the wrong man. I have known some ministers to be defeated because they have lost their early confidence in Christianity and their early belief in the specific mission of the Church.

We may see the weakness of Protestant leadership in the

fact that so many ministers come to follow the lines of least resistance in their forms of activity. They may continue to be busy about many things, but they may become victims of routine, with no capacity to plan their lives, to study or to think. It is not altogether the minister's fault but it is a symbol of his predicament that too often books are a luxury whereas gasoline is a necessity.

The leaders of Protestantism have failed to make much impression on the class and racial prejudices of their constituencies. The results of the intensive teaching of the social gospel among the clergy themselves have been disappointing in the Church at large. One indication of this is that during the past twelve years some of the immediate social goals of this teaching have been realized in the nation but this has been accomplished in the teeth of the opposition of the majority of white, middle-class Protestants. The pressures of class interest have been only slightly modified by religious teaching.

There is much cause for pessimism concerning the Church if one counts up its limitations as we have been asked to do. This is especially true if one omits, as must be done here, the glorious chapters in the history of the contemporary church or if one ignores for the moment the faithful and creative work that is done by ministers and laymen in thousands of churches. Always from the days when Paul saw the best and the worst in the churches that he served there have been these contrasts in the life of the Church. But deeper than these contrasts there is the fact that the Church bears constant witness to the truth by which it is corrected and even in its darkest days it mediates the Spirit of God that is ever seeking to transform it.

Further Reading

Niebuhr, Richard. *The Social Sources of Denominationalism.* New York: Henry Holt and Company, 1929.

Pope, Liston. *Millhands and Preachers.* New Haven: Yale University Press. 1942.

Visser 't Hooft, W. A. *The Wretchedness and Greatness of the Church.* Tr. Dorothy Mackie and Hugh Martin. London: Student Christian Movement Press, 1944.

Visser 't Hooft, W. A., and Oldham, J .H. *The Church and Its Function in Society.* Chicago: Willett, Clark & Company, 1937.

PART III. The Present Task

CHAPTER VII

Necessary Reorientations in Thought and Life

Luman J. Shafer

CHAPTER VIII

The Vocation of the Christian Today

Elmer G. Homrighausen

7

NECESSARY REORIENTATIONS IN THOUGHT AND LIFE

Luman J. Shafer

Introduction. 1. Contrasting temper in the Church and the community, and the reorientation required: attitudes toward truth: restatement of creeds, needed tests, the preacher and the sermon, religion and science. 2. Christianity and the family: family centered conceptions and programs. 3. The relation of the ideal to the practical: the responsibility of the Church for a Christian society, the guiding principle. 4. The parochial and the ecumenical in the local church.

If there is one thing fixed in human life it is the fact of change. Life is never static. Growth and change—sometimes violent and revolutionary, but more often gradual and evolutionary—are qualities of living organisms, whether of men or institutions. But there is bound to be disparity in the rate of change and as a result there is a constant tension between an organism and its environment. Furthermore, inertia is a powerful factor and in the attempt to avoid the effort involved in reorientation the living organism tends to become static and thus more and more at odds with its environment, until it may be dispensed with entirely. This is particularly true of institutions.

It is, therefore, not out of place to suggest that there is need for reorientation in the life and thought of the Church. To do so does not imply that the fundamental core of the life of the Church, its vital force and inner nature, must be changed. But it does mean that that inner core of life, in order to become more really alive and vital, needs constantly to readjust to meet changing conditions. Not to do so is to deny its very nature as a living organism, the true Body of Christ in the world. Not to bring about constant reorientation is to become static and this is a quality not of life, but of death.

An exhaustive study of the kind of reorientation required in the thought and life of the Church would involve a careful examination of the environment in the American community today, including governing ideas and ideals, changing mores and the general trend of mass thinking. This would need then to be brought over against the thought and life of the Church; and the effort made to discover where the lag in church life is to be found, in what respects this is inherent in the unchanging nature of the Church and in what respects reorientation is possible and necessary. It is obviously impossible to do this in one brief chapter. We shall have to confine our discussion to some rather obvious generalizations which will be apparent without the research which would be a prerequisite to a thorough study of the problem.

1. CONTRASTING TEMPER IN THE CHURCH AND THE COMMUNITY, AND THE REORIENTATION REQUIRED

It is apparent to anyone that the average person living in America today finds a striking contrast between the approach to life with which he is ordinarily familiar in his various contacts and the attitude or approach which he finds within the Church. There is here a quite different orientation. The timbre or tone quality is one to which his ears have not been accustomed in his normal contacts.

Attitudes toward truth

In the Church he finds that truth is thought of as something definite. It can be made explicit and can be defined in precise language. It is so real that he would know it if he met it on the street. It must be laid hold of actively and precisely and held with conviction. There is a clear line of division between truth and falsehood, and what is not true is false. He finds the preacher dealing with "truths" of this sort, in a rather lighthearted way it seems to him, in twenty minutes on a Sunday morning.

The society from which he comes, however, is set in a drastically different climate. There everything is tentative and subject to the final check of experience. What is true is not the primary consideration. The question stressed is, does it work? In most situations the issue of true or false, right or wrong, never really comes to the surface at all. Everything but the practical consideration is pushed into the background. Truth is not something to which a fixed and final name can be attached, but, if considered at all, it is viewed as a constantly shifting factor which has to be held tentatively and made use of so long as it gets results. In fact, it is positively suspect until, by demonstration, it has been shown to work.

In the Church the assumption seems to be that the good life consists in orientation to truth. Ethical conduct flows *out from* such orientation. The ethical standards are thought of as something "given." They must be treated with respect and their operation is unchanging and inexorable. What is true is wholesome and healing; what is false is unhealthy and destructive. In the society in which the worshiper on a Sunday morning lives his daily life, however, the facts as he meets them are supposed somehow to yield their own moral purpose. It is not his business to impose upon the "facts" with which he deals a purpose which proceeds from some supposed moral imperative of the God the preacher is talking about, but he expects each situation, if viewed on a purely factual basis, to yield its own guiding principle. The facts of themselves are supposed to "secrete a moral purpose."

There is also something dogmatic about the preacher's presentation. He seems bound by an inner conviction that does not permit critical examination. He seems to be presenting his material on a take-it-or-leave-it basis. The hearer, however, is saturated with a spirit which shies away from anything that is stated dogmatically and is set forth in the form of fixed principles to be accepted. Scientific studies have uncovered a vast and mysterious universe and have revealed how little is really known about it. There has resulted a kind of reticence with regard to truth. A hypothesis held today may be found to be untenable tomorrow as new facts are discovered, and what the ultimate truth may be, if indeed there be any such, is not clear. The truth about life appears to be too vast and obscure to be stated. All we can do is to find out what works and be content with that until something more workable comes along.

Another aspect of this modern temper is the large place given to method and technique. From the approach which makes workability primary and truth incidental to use, there is a natural shift to greater emphasis on the method or technique used in putting a supposed principle or truth to work. Often, in actual experience, the method appears to be as important as the new principle or truth discovered. It is the "know-how" in the practical application of the principle of atomic fission which is the real secret today in international circles, not the "principle" itself. Thus, in common thinking, method or technique is erected into a kind of an absolute. The reasoning runs like this, "Once you get the know-how, you can do almost anything. You need not be too much troubled about matters of fact, or matters of principle. All that you really need to know is how to operate to get the results you need." *How to Win Friends and Influence People* is a classic example of this temper in modern life.

The spirit which seems to guide the vast apparatus of modern advertising again illustrates the point. The truth is regarded as comparatively unimportant. It is the method that counts. What you have to say must not be too far removed from a factual basis, but the desired public acceptance is to be attained not by the weight of the facts themselves so much as by the way the supposed facts are presented. The important thing is to surround the statement which you wish to be believed or the object which you wish to sell with the proper psychological trappings. In other words, the idea seems to be that people do not believe, or rush out to buy your product, or work out the desired program of activities because of their inherent truth; but because you have made them *want* to believe or you have used the art of suggestion so skillfully that subconsciously they are bound to accept what you tell them. You draw a beautiful landscape or a charming girl and associate it with your product, so that the pleasurable sensation of the picture will unconsciously be transferred to the article which you wish to sell. Or you repeat the magic word as many times as possible in a musical setting with suitable phrases associated with joyous achievement and let the psychological law of suggestibility do the rest. Thus technique supplants truth.

From even this sketch of the temper of our day the reader will have no difficulty in recognizing it in his own experience. The question remains whether or not the disparity between the feel of things inside the Church and the feel of things outside constitutes a challenge to reorientation in thought within the Church. There is a sense in which the modern temper is the result of a process of secularization. To modify the thought life of the Church to meet it would only tend to secularize the Church itself. It can and must be said that this modern temper is shallow. It is too "smooth" and basically insincere to be taken over seriously by the Church. It must sooner or later become "ashes in the mouth" because it is out of touch with ultimate realities and these realities will catch up with people where they live and make them ask questions to which the Church has the answers. It is precisely this kind of paganism that the Church in every age has come to redeem. It must also be contended that there is a difference between the intuitional value judgment of religion and the measurable facts of science. These values must, in the nature of the case, be apprehended by other methods than those developed in scientific procedures. It must be made clear that the scientist is a man and must act on some guiding principles of conduct and that so long as these are held only tentatively they possess little dynamic for life. It must be pointed out that even the scientist accepts certain basic truths about the universe not subject to proof by the methods of measurement as, for example, the conviction that the universe always acts in a reasonable and consistent manner and is therefore subject to repetitional and statistical handling.

But is it enough to do only this? Are there not points at

which the Church should and must adjust itself to the modern temper?

Creeds must be rewritten

In the first place, we should be prepared to state the religious truths embodied in the ancient creeds in thought patterns that are understandable to the modern mind. The great creeds and confessions came into being as an attempt to make clear in the language of that day the great facts of the Christian faith. Not to restate them in modern language and modern patterns of thought comes dangerously near to confessing that the faith that produced them in the first place is not as vital as it was when they came into being. It is absurd to suppose that with the radical changes that have taken place in the last two centuries a statement of any fact or truth can be adequately made in the phraseology of two or four hundred years ago. If the truth of Christianity is living and imperative, as we believe it to be, its vitality must be made real in the terms of the day in which we live. That is not to say that in doing this we should change the truth itself. What is essentially true in Christianity must be susceptible to statement in modern terms and with the use of the thought patterns of today, or it cannot be true. Truth is eternal but its expression and its mental framework must change as men's minds change. Water is always water but it must take the shape of the vessel into which it is poured. Truth to be convincing must be poured through the mind, and its particular expression will be modified as the mind pattern changes.

Tests need to be applied

It should be hardly necessary to add, also, that the essential truths of Christianity can and must be subject to the pragmatic test. The conviction with which the preacher presents the great truths of the Christian faith will be strengthened, not lessened, if they are firmly grounded in experience and subject to the test of practical usefulness. They are not true because they are useful but they must be useful if they are true. The "facts" do not secrete the moral purpose, but moral purpose becomes most luminous when it is brought over against the facts of experience. The physical fact of one world and the psychological facts of fear and self-interest will not of themselves create a humane world order. But the truth that God made of one blood all nations for to dwell on the face of the earth becomes most vivid when the actual situation in the modern world is faced with clarity. It then becomes clear that the development of real brotherhood is the price of human survival in the modern world. The truth will work and just because it is true nothing else will.

Furthermore, because religious truth must meet the pragmatic test, the Church needs to develop more honest ways of finding out how and why it works, and if it is not getting results the reasons for its failure. While the current emphasis on method as of supreme importance with the consequent lack of interest in moral principle is an aberration, which cannot serve as a guide for the Church, the Church errs on the other side in paying too little attention to the practical working out of its teaching. There must be a better developed system of tests to show, for instance, whether preaching really gets results in changed lives and renewed character. The preacher says, "I preached a sermon on that last Sunday." The irreverent has a right to remark, "So what? Did it get anywhere? What were the results?" We need to look upon the whole activity of the Church as an educational process, and we should never be content until we know that what we are doing is proving itself in life.

That is quite a different thing, to be sure, from saying that a thing is true because it works, or that its truth depends on or is proven by its workability; but if it be true, as we are convinced, then it must work and we need to know how and why, or if not why not. Technique and method alone cannot be trusted for results, but without suitable techniques of application to life the best of truths will prove sterile.

The preacher and the sermon

The Protestant churches are dominated by the sermon and the preacher. In part this is a matter of conviction and strength, for "the preaching of the Word" is essential to church life. But in our time it has become subject to needed reforms.

The preacher deals with great truths, and it should be possible to hold unshaken one's conviction of Christian truth and, at the same time, present it with a sensitive understanding of the fact that one is dealing with profound mysteries, and that no one statement—certainly not one made in twenty minutes on a Sunday morning—can exhaust the vast possibilities of its full-orbed immensity. Real conviction should not issue in bombastic arrogance but in suitable personal modesty and decorum. The reticence of the scientifically trained person and his dislike of dogmatisms should be respected. While holding firmly to the value judgments of religious faith the preacher should exhibit a similar modesty in his handling of the great facts of his religion.

There should be more opportunity for a comeback at the preacher. The whole atmosphere of the church service, including the sermon, offers little outlet for individual opinion or question. Of course, the church service cannot be turned into a forum for discussion, although that method is being widely used to good advantage in other parts of the church's program, but even the sermon at the services of worship should be couched in terms suitable for discussion and, what is more important, presented in such a way as to suggest a willingness to hear others' opinions. In some places midweek meetings for question and discussion of the Sunday morning theme have been found practicable.

Certainly some opportunity must be offered to those who have doubts and questions. It should be frankly assumed that the preaching and teaching of the Church will become vital only as it meets the intellectual demands of the people and is clearly and firmly integrated with the kind of thinking which they encounter in other places in society. The truths of Christian faith should be so presented as to invite question and full opportunity should be given, particularly to young people, for them to express their opinions and bring their questionings forward frankly.

Is it not about time to get rid of the "flowery" sermon and the pulpit voice? A young chemist asked recently why the preacher talked so differently from anybody else. He said, "You can always tell a preacher when you tune in on the radio even before you get the drift of his theme." Is there any particular reason why the presentation of Christian truth should be on a different basis from the exposition of any other set of facts? In any case, there can be no doubt that the modern temper requires factual statements as brief and succinct as possible. The language of the newspaper, the magazine and the radio is direct and simple. The radio announcer is intimate and matter-of-fact. A radio announcer once said to a preacher after he had finished his address over the radio, "You don't sound like a preacher." Well, why in the name of common sense should anyone sound like a preacher? The important thing is to have something to say and to say it as directly, as succinctly and as simply as it can be said. In this respect the modern attitude is sound: at this point we in the Church need a good deal of self-examination.

Religion and science

All this is, to be sure, one aspect of a larger problem of reorientation which must be faced if the Church is to meet the temper of our day on anything but a superficial basis. The creeds cannot be rewritten in terms of mere translation into modern speech. The pragmatic, secularistic temper of present-day society cannot be really met until the theological viewpoint and the scientific viewpoint are fused into one intellectually consistent whole. This cannot be done by making theology the end product of science, and certainly not by confining theology to one realm and science to another. The atmosphere is clearer today than it was twenty-five years ago. The limitation of science to the discovery of values which are subject to measurement and controlled test is better recognized today. There is also increasing recognition of the converse fact, that there are areas of value which cannot be discovered by the scientific method. It is more apparent now that the whole discipline of science is based on presuppositions which are not subject to scientific demonstration. The need of other approaches to truth than that of measurement and test alone is thus more generally recognized. But it is still true that there is little fusing of the two. Each discipline moves pretty much under its own steam. There is slight intellectual fraternization between them and such conversations as there are across the no man's land which divides them are still scarcely intelligible on either side. What is needed is the frank recognition that Christianity is and must be a total world view and the challenge is not one of reconciliation of two independent disciplines but a reconstruction of Christian interpretation so as to include all of truth. This is a task of major proportions and it is foolhardy to think, as some apparently do, that that job has already been done.

2. CHRISTIANITY AND THE FAMILY

Reorientation in Church life is needed in regard to the *temper* of our times; it is also needed in regard to the structure of our society. Later we shall deal with other areas, but at present consider especially the family. We need seriously to raise the question whether Christianity in America has not been assimilated to a secular individualism springing from the Renaissance and the influence of Rousseau upon modern democracy to the neglect of the family and the corporate nature of society. The center of gravity for Christianity in our churches is certainly not the family or the corporate group but the individual or groups composed of isolated individuals. The net effect of Christianity has thus been to contribute to the atomization of modern life rather than to develop social solidarity and stability.

Following the trend of American life we have individualized and personalized Christianity until the family as such comes into the church program only incidentally. Our church schools are organized on the psychological principle of different age levels; the young people's program is built around the young people as a distinct group. There are women's societies and men's clubs, business women's groups and so on. Almost everything we do tends to atomize the family. At the same time we are confronted with the social fact that the family in America is disintegrating. Marriages are extremely unstable and the family unit as a real factor in society is becoming increasingly unimportant.

It is well to observe that in the older societies which have persisted for thousands of years the family is central. The individual may be undervalued and in some cases his interests may be unduly sacrificed to the welfare and needs of the family, but the survival of these older civilizations is in large part due to the central place given to the family as a corporate entity of paramount importance. It is probably also true to say that the stability of the family has been maintained in these cultures because religion has been closely identified with it. In India, China and Japan ancestor worship is a function of the family and religious training is carried on largely in the home.

The missionary in these countries becomes keenly aware of the extent to which Christianity as he has acquired it in America has been assimilated to the individualistic society of the Western world. As he presents it on an individualistic basis, he sees it separating the individual from his family. He finds that Christianity, along with industrialization and other factors introduced from the West, contributes to the loosening of family ties and the breakup of these cultures. This weakness has been taken account of more recently in India, where, in the mass movement, families are brought into the fellowship of the Church as units and the process of disintegration has to that extent been arrested. But, by and large, the contact of Christianity with the family solidarity of the ancient East or the tribal solidarity of the primitive African has been on an individualistic basis. Thus the extent to which Christianity has been assimilated to the individualistic and atomistic society of the West has been thrown into sharp focus against the family-centered cultures of the older societies.

Christianity must become family-centered

This experience has brought us up sharply against some very important facts. History has proven that cultures grounded on the family have the ability to persist. It is not yet clear whether a society not so grounded can long survive. Furthermore, in these cultures where the family is stable and central, religion is a family matter. In our society, where religion is based on the individual or on the group composed of isolated individuals, the family is disintegrating.

What is urgently needed is not a change in the method of approach to meet the altered situation as outlined in the first section of this chapter. What is required, if we are to stay the atomization of society and the disintegration of the home, is a determined effort to recover a more nearly true perspective of the nature of Christianity as a cultural factor. It is clear that unless this is done by some force in society, our Western culture has little chance of survival. Christianity arose in a family-centered culture. While its appeal is to individual decision and individual responsibility, the family is also integral to the Christian system. It is therefore imperative that this be more clearly recognized. Christianity needs again to be grounded on the family and the family must be recovered as a center of religious instruction and religious ceremony.

What has happened is that the overemphasis on the individual in Protestantism has brought about the almost complete secularization of the family. Family prayers have gradually disappeared. Even grace at meals is becoming more and more uncommon. In fact, few family ceremonies remain, either of a religious or nonreligious character. Even where marriage is performed by the minister it is an isolated rite. In the Orient the marriage ceremony is an integral part of regular family ceremonies connected with worship of the ancestors. With us, it has no relation whatever to any usual family religious ceremonies.

Bringing Christianity to the home

It is easy enough to state the problem but unfortunately it is more difficult to know what to do about it. In some sections of the country families still attend the church services as a unit. In most places, however, the Sunday morning church school has pretty effectively dispensed with that custom. In many churches, church family nights have been developed to meet this problem. But, by and large, very little that is effective is being done. The end to be sought, in any case, should be clear. It is not enough to bring the families together to the church. Religion and the ceremonies of religion must be brought back to the home.

More use should be made of the great religious festivals of the year. General services in the church on these high days are undoubtedly desirable, but it is questionable if even this is as important as that the family gatherings on these days should be made religious in character. Thanksgiving, Christmas Day, New Year's Eve, and other high days should be met religiously in the home and suitable rites and ceremonies for them should be developed and encouraged. General family gatherings for anniversaries are also occasions for religious exercises in the home. Were this done, Christian people would find these days all the more pleasurable and the family as a divinely ordained institution would be more clearly recognized. There should be religious ceremonies connected with the building of a house and the entrance into a new home. The first plowing in the country might well be consecrated by a religious service. Home-leaving and home-coming after a long absence should also have a religious recognition. In the early days of the war a mother voiced her feeling of disappointment that there had been no special observance of the departure of her son for the service. She felt the need of a communion service to consecrate his going. Here again whatever sort of ceremony is held should be carried out in the home and not in the church. There are many occasions where such a home service might be employed in commemoration of leave-taking or home-coming and special rituals, which could be carried out in the home, should be developed and their use actively encouraged. In short, family occurrences of importance should be religiously recognized in the family, as is the case in all countries where the family as an institution is still a vital part of society.

Religious education should also be centered in the home. There is considerable weight behind the suggestion that the church school on Sunday morning should be replaced by a program of religious education which would begin in the home and end in weekday classes in the church. This may be impractical, but unless something like it is done the home will not become what it should be, the center and fountainhead of religious experience, and the home itself will continue to be what it is today, a secularized and, therefore, a disintegrating institution.

3. THE RELATION OF THE IDEAL TO THE PRACTICAL

Another problem of reorientation in the life of the Church, which is always present, is particularly important today because of the emphasis on the practical in modern society and because members of the churches are taking an ever larger part in seeking to apply the Christian gospel in social and political life: how shall the ideal be related to the practical effectively and with conviction and power.

The Gospel comes to us as something "given" and is stated in terms of the ideal. "Be ye perfect, even as your Father in heaven is perfect," is the key to its spirit. But the kingdom of heaven is viewed as something to be sought here and now as well as in the future. The Christian is under compulsion to strive to attain the ideals of the kingdom in his own life and in society. The more completely he is dedicated to the fulfillment of the *ideal* terms of the Gospel as they affect him and society the more profound is his conviction and the more determined his will to action.

But, in the nature of the case, when this will to action becomes related to a particular social or political situation it becomes apparent that action must be taken at a lower level than the ideal if there is to be any effective action. The actual situation, being a human situation, presents elements which are far from ideal. In other words, the ideal is always so far in advance of the actual situation that to attempt a complete practical construction in terms of it would be, in effect, to secure little immediate modification of the situation even in the direction of the ideal sought. On the other hand, to whittle down the ideal to the point where it can actually function in the existing situation seems to the Christian to be a compromise and, therefore, he tends to lose conviction and drive in securing the only change that is practicable at the moment.

Has Christianity a responsibility for creating a Christian society?

This problem has been obviated in the past in the Church by contending in various ways that it is not the business of the Church to attempt to reform human institutions or Christianize a secular society. In one view the social application of the Gospel has been thought of as futile since the human situation is so involved in human sin as to be beyond redemption this side of the end of the age. In another view the social application of the Gospel is irrelevant to the function of the Church since by divine ordering there is one domain for the Church and another for the State. This latter, of course, was the position in Germany and a neutral attitude was taken toward the Nazi state so long as it did not attempt to enter the particular field of the Church. Still another position is that it is the sole business of the Church to proclaim the ideal and leave the individual Christian to work out the implications of the Gospel in his daily life as best he may.

Any or all of these attitudes would make the problem which we have raised irrelevant. It is our contention, however, that detachment from society and social change is impossible. The traditional position of the German churches toward the state has had disastrous consequences in recent years and is being radically modified on the continent of Europe. The experience of the churches of the Netherlands during the war has again vindicated the conviction that the whole of society is under God and is of vital concern to the Church.

If it be considered futile to attempt to change society, in the last analysis it becomes futile to change the individual. For the individual is so bound up in the social and political environment and so affected by it that action which does not seek to make his life in all its relationships as Christian as possible comes very close to being no action at all. If Christian action is thought of as purely within the individual, confined largely to his inner life, this interior realm is so much a part of the social milieu and so controlled by the interplay of all the forces of the environment, that he is forced to do something about his environment if he is to succeed in maintaining a measure of Christian life within. It is the business of the Church to follow through and give such direction to action, both individual and social, that the Christian ideal shall in some measure become operative in all of life. It is hard to see how individual Christian action can be expected unless, at the same time, Christian social and political action is demanded.

A guiding principle

We return, then, to the problem which this presents in the life of the Church. How is conviction to be maintained for the less than the ideal which must be sought in social and political action, if action is to be taken at all? One very excellent recent example of this problem in the life of the Church is afforded by the movement for a world order. From the early days of the work of the Commission on a Just and Durable Peace of the Federal Council of Churches this problem presented itself. Was the Commission to state its program in terms of the ideal world order which seems to be called for by the Gospel or should it aim at the next practicable steps? The method followed was, first, to state a series of guiding principles which seemed to flow from the Gospel, and then to follow them with six political propositions, which came more closely to grips with the existing situation. The six propositions aimed at much less than the guiding principles but were considered to be in harmony with them and were viewed as immediate steps to be taken in order to move toward the ideal. These propositions were severely criticized as being too near the actual situation, too "unideal" in character and as giving away too much. In other words, there were large groups of Christians who lost conviction when the general ideals were brought to bear upon the real situation and when it was sought to put them to work in the only terms practicable in existing political conditions.

This problem became even more acute when at the Cleveland Conference of the Commission of January, 1945, a representative group of Christians faced the necessity of action on the Dumbarton Oaks Proposals which were afterwards developed into the Charter of the United Nations. It was perfectly clear that the proposals fell lamentably short of the ideal and even though amended would still be far from an implementation of the Christian Guiding Principles adopted by the Commission earlier. They were not a complete fulfillment even of the six political propositions. At the same time, it was clear that the new world order must follow in general the outline of the Dumbarton Oaks Proposals if it was to be created at all, and this was, of course, in doubt at that time. There were those who favored rejecting the proposals on the ground that they were imperfect and that, therefore, Christians should not become identified with them. Others felt that we should seek through amendment to improve the organization and throw all our weight behind it as the only *practical* step looking toward world co-operation. To have attempted perfection at that time and to have rejected the Dumbarton Oaks proposals might have lost the movement for the creation of the United Nations organization altogether.

The action that was taken at Cleveland was as follows:

> We recommend that the churches support the Dumbarton Oaks Proposals as an important step in the direction of world cooperation but, since we do not approve of them in their entirety as they now stand, we urge the following measures for their improvement.

And then nine amendments were proposed. The principle which governed this action was stated as follows:

> Christians must act in situations as they exist and must decide what God's will demands of them there. At all times they must keep the ultimate goals clearly in view but they have equal responsibility to work out attainable steps toward these goals and support them. An idealism which does not accept the discipline of the achievable may lose its power for good and ultimately lend aid to forces with whose purposes it cannot agree.

The tension between the ideal, as ideal, and the ideal as actively at work in an actual situation which has been apparent throughout the work of this important Commission is an excellent illustration of the dilemma which is constantly confronted in the life of the Church. The crux of the problem is how to maintain drive and conviction in support of measures which are less than the ideal but which represent the only way the ideal can function practically in the existing social and political situation. Full conviction can be mustered for the Gospel as "given," for the ideal kingdom of heaven, but great difficulty is encountered when the actual human situation is faced and action on the human level is called for,

This difficulty largely arises from the fact that the problem has not been squarely faced. The fear of compromise is grounded in a sound purpose not to dilute the purity of the Gospel and its ideal. Over against this must be put the fact that action must and will be taken, and either the Christian will throw his weight behind the immediate next step which he is convinced will move the whole situation in the direction of a more Christian society or, so far as he is concerned, the whole process moves without the aid of any Christian purpose. Much of social action is taken on purely secular grounds because the Christian, in his fear of compromise, takes no definite Christian position and lets the whole matter go by default.

The Church needs also to carry through with the Christian

layman in his day by day decisions. In the view that it is the sole business of the Church to proclaim the ideal and then to leave the individual Christian to work out the implications of the Gospel as best he may, the individual Christian is left without comfort or guidance precisely at the point where action takes place. In that case the Christian is almost compelled to develop a duality of experience. His Christian ideals are confined to his inner, personal life and his life in society becomes completely secularized. Or, if he tries to modify the social situation to meet his Christian principles, he does not move in this area with conviction and power but is constantly weakened by a feeling that in his action he is compromising his ideals.

What is needed is a clearer recognition of this whole problem and a more definite implementation of practical procedures. The experience of the Commission on a Just and Durable Peace should be generalized and more largely used. We need to recognize that "Christians must act in situations as they exist" and that it is possible to find out what "God's will demands of him there." If this can be done, the Christian can then act with equal conviction in the practical situation because God's will is present for him there as well as in the remote ideal. Whatever the answer is, it is imperative that we face this problem so that the same drive that gathers around the ideals themselves can be made available for the "next steps" in action.

4. THE PAROCHIAL AND THE ECUMENICAL IN THE LOCAL CHURCH

There are two currents in the life of the Church which run counter to each other and which need to be brought together if we are to meet the challenge of our day. One of these is the ecumenical movement, the tendency for churches of all lands to draw together in common fellowship. At heart this is the outreach of the basic belief in the universality of Christianity, its supranational and supraracial character. It is the outgrowth of the missionary movement, based likewise on the conviction that Christianity if true for us is true for all men and must, in the nature of the case, be shared with all. The current which moves in the opposite direction is the trend to parochialism. It tends to enhance the importance of the local church and the local situation to the exclusion of interests outside the immediate parish. The latter attitude may be regarded as the natural down-drag of human nature which is primarily concerned with personal matters and which is most aglow when the individual himself or things which he can call his own are in the center of the picture. This natural and valuable human trait is often unconsciously prostituted by the local minister and made to feed into the glory and achievements of the local congregation and, incidentally, of course, to enhance the value of his own leadership. This tendency to build everything around the local minister and his leadership is a serious weakness of the Protestant Church, for, in many cases, what we have is not a real church at all but a group of people motivated almost exclusively by the same sort of narrow group loyalty which activates ordinary secular groups. The adulation of "our" minister and the kind of purely personal allegiance which is developed is often so parochial as to be almost nauseating.

Where this is surmounted it is often done by creating the larger loyalty to the particular denomination, so that the local group now has an added element of self-satisfaction in knowing that it belongs to a going concern of larger proportions. The growing efficiency of denominational central organization is a marked development of recent decades. The danger is that this will develop a denominational solidarity which will not enhance in the local parish the sense of the universality of the Gospel, but rather will strengthen the parochial and minister to the self-centeredness of the local church.

It must be confessed that the ecumenical movement, while grounded on the universality of the Gospel and accepted in a general sort of way by many of the rank and file of the Church membership, is still largely a movement "at the top." It will necessarily remain so until in the local church the sense of the universal fellowship of all Christians and the responsibility of each Christian for sharing his faith with all men everywhere become the dominating spirit of everything that is done locally. The parochial will always stifle the sense of the universal unless the universality of the Gospel becomes a dominating motive. The ecumenical spirit cannot be added to the parochial as something peripheral. It must dominate and become central if it is to have any vital meaning.

Perhaps there is nothing more important than this in the life of the local church today. It is important not so much because the ecumenical movement must be grounded in the local church if it is to be effective. It is important primarily because of the nature of the Gospel itself. If the local church fails at this point its whole life is truncated and crippled. But it is also important because of the kind of world in which we must live today. A Church which is not aware that we are living in "one world" will shortly cease to be effective in any important way even in the local community, for we are moving into a social situation where local problems and world problems are being rapidly telescoped. As a consequence, local problems must be solved in the light of, and along with, world problems if they are to be solved at all. Not only has the universality of the Gospel "come to the kingdom for such a day as this," but the world situation itself demands that the Church become world-minded if it is to be effective at all.

Probably the best way to create an ecumenically-minded Church is through the service of worship. No service of worship should be allowed to pass which does not at some point lift the congregation out of its local and parochial milieu into the ecumenical fellowship and confront it with the needs of the world of men. It need not always be conspicuous but if it is definitely in the mind of the minister as he prepares his services and is reflected in the hymns, or in his choice of illustrations for his sermon or even in the notes in the bulletin, it will have its effect upon the congregation. It is most important that it be evidenced as the minister leads his congregation in prayer. There is a congregation in New York State, more than normally parochial, that in a little more than a year was completely changed in its attitude by a conscious effort of this sort on the part of the minister. The local church can be made ecumenical in its outlook if the leadership of the church wants it that way: no minister can evade his responsibility.

For suggestions for further reading, see pages 224 and 225.

8

THE VOCATION OF THE CHRISTIAN TODAY

Elmer G. Homrighausen

1. Social tensions and the individual. 2. The concept of Christian vocation: life under God. 3. The decline of the sense of vocation: varied concepts, the secularization of vocation. 4. The basis and nature of the Christian's vocation: sin and vocation, the redeemed vocation, the centrality of love, Christian vocation and the world. 5. Aspects of the Christian's vocation: service, evangelism, work, family, Church, citizenship, economic life, race, social responsibility. 6. Disciplines: the Bible, worship, fellowship, good works, the common life under God. 7. Resources: Word, Gospel and Providence, the Church.

In the foregoing chapters the reader has been introduced to the various aspects of the general theme of this volume—*The Gospel, the Church and the World*. The burden of this chapter has to do with the nature, resources and tasks of the individual Christian in our day. Simply put, the question to be answered is: What is the "vocation" of the Christian?

1. SOCIAL TENSIONS AND THE INDIVIDUAL

While human beings are bound together in the "bundle of life," the individual is after all the basic unit of personal existence. We make no defense of our concern for the individual. We are aware of the fact that the major issues which now agitate us are social in character. International, race and class relations are dominant today. The individual feels the impact of these tensions; and, to a great degree, his personal problems result from them. It is no longer possible to consider personality apart from the social environment of which it is a part.

The future is fraught with terrific tensions for the Christian citizen, parent, child, youth, scholar. It will be concerned with the establishment of a corporate order which will provide the framework in which the individual may hope for a more ordered life. However, a stable social framework is not necessary for the Christian individual; the Christian life is, when realistically conceived, always lived in an abnormal situation which is often inimical to the Christian faith and life. The Christian, too, partakes of the abnormality of society, since he is still a sinner.

One of the chief causes of neurosis today is the situation which the individual confronts. His life cannot be lived in a vacuum. He is interrelated with the human situation. He is not only a victim of the disintegration of an established order, he has also lost his meaningfulness. Professor Hocking speaks of two realms of experience, namely, that of public order and that of private order. The former refers to the social and natural order and the latter to the personal. Modern man no longer finds himself in possession of inner order, because he has so largely shifted the center of his life to the external order. This outer framework is now in the process of disruption. This outer order was never intended to give man security, for it has always been subject to change. Since man is in great need of coming to himself, and of finding himself in the order of God, the emphasis upon the personal and individual must, it seems to us, receive great attention today. It is doubtful whether any kind of rehabilitation or habilitation of an external order will be able to provide man with the necessary ground and purpose of life.

We must take into account the fact that there are in evidence today trends toward solitariness and escape from the social order. Despairing of the situation, some are taking to the consolations of mysticism. Without discounting the necessity of solitude and mysticism (of the right sort!) in the Christian life, we cannot agree with the extreme advocates of this position.

We must also recognize the fact that there are abroad attempts to deal with our tragic situation in the spirit of the superman. Taking hold of life by violent hands, some have sought so to master nature and society with a view to liquidating untoward elements in the modern life-situation. Again, we admit that while the Christian is to have dominion, we cannot accept the basic theology of the modern superman.

There are still others, quite intelligent, who have adopted a steely stoicism. Resigning themselves to the inevitable, irremedial situation, they advocate an integration of the individual around the laws of nature and society. They seek to live a life of culture and reasonable social concern by the law of disinterestedness. This solution to the problem of man's vocation leaves much to be desired.

The Christian, who has a sense of vocation under God, pursues none of these courses. His life is not at the mercy of an impersonal Fate; nor does he cultivate the "spiritual life" in isolation from nature or society; nor does he seek by sheer human strength of body and mind to transcend his tragic situation. He confronts life in the here and now in the power of the Gospel of Jesus Christ.

2. THE CONCEPT OF CHRISTIAN VOCATION

The term "vocation" simply means: "a person's sense of being called to a task." This definition, taken from the little Oxford Dictionary, needs qualification if it is to be used in a Christian sense. Most people have the idea that a vocation is a profession, or type of work. Hence, one is in the medical or the legal vocation if he is a physician or a lawyer.

But the meaning of vocation in its broader sense, as used by the Reformers, does not limit a Christian's vocation to the ministry. Calvin, for instance, did not limit the term to a particular form of religious work. He believed that every Christian had a vocation, not only because he was called by God in Christ to a life of fellowship with Himself, but because he was called to serve God in whatever work he was engaged. The whole round of common tasks is related to the Christian's life with God. God's will is not to be found in isolation; it is related to every moment of the common life. The "glory of God," which men are to seek, is not separated from life and work in the home and community. The glory of God may and must be promoted in the family, the daily task and the everyday life. Every aspect of the world's work is thus given a somewhat sacramental status.

Life under God

The whole life of the Christian, whatever his social position or professional labor, is to be under the sovereignty of God. There is no separation between the religious life and the daily life. This conception has little affinity with the asceticism of the Middle Ages which regarded the religious calling as the only true vocation. It has no affinity whatever with modern secularism, which sees the religious in the secular. Nor has it any affinity with a type of dualistic Christianity which separates the religious and the secular into two unrelated spheres.

It is often thought that this conception of vocation fails to take the good of the individual and the happiness of society into account. An extreme emphasis upon the glory of God may fail to grant man freedom to choose and change his work; it may not provide for the human factor in determining what is good. However, the question may be asked: How does man know what is good for himself or society? The will of God is the highest good of men, and in the light of that will it is my duty to determine what I ought to do in the lesser goods of life.

This conception does not involve a lack of concern for the good of society or the happiness of the individual. Rather, it rejects the idea that man is the measure of all things in favor of the conception that man is created in the image of God, redeemed by the divine action of God through His Son, and empowered through the Holy Spirit to a new life in Christ.

Calvin writes that "God has appointed to all their particular duties in different spheres of life. . . . Every individual's line of life, therefore, is, as it were, a post assigned him by the Lord, that he may not wander about in uncertainty all his days." He continues by saying that that life is best regulated which is directed to this mark. Every individual who is persuaded that his burden is laid upon him by God will the better be able to do his duty, and he will be better able to bear up under the vicissitudes which befall human existence. And every task will have its own glory, even that which has to do with lowly things, because it is highly esteemed in the sight of God.

It can be argued that a rigid application of this conception of vocation might lead to a sanction of the status quo, and it might be interpreted in such a way as to disparage enterprise. But Calvin did not so conceive vocationalism. Luther may have given a somewhat different emphasis to the doctrine, by assigning a more passive role to man in the economy of an ordered society. Luther's emphasis upon grace and his rather pessimistic conception of history and the function of the state may have influenced his conception of the life of the Christian in the world of affairs. But Calvin stressed the sovereignty of God in all spheres of life. Man must respond to the call of God, and as a steward he must exercise his responsibility in the choice and exercise of a vocation.

Protestantism stresses the equality of all believers before God. This is the basis of its democracy which rejects hierarchies of both Church and State. All labor is looked upon as dignified, though there are different kinds to be performed. But beneath all these kinds of work, there is what Horace Bushnell expressed: "Every Man's Life a Plan of God." This "plan of God" is not only the plan of salvation, but a plan which includes man in the divine economy of human affairs.

When life is seen in the light of its divine vocation, the secular and the sacred are not two mutually exclusive realms of concern. To be sure, there is a distinction to be made between a place devoted to purely Christian uses and a place that is not so used. However, a church building is not meant to separate Christianity from a home, for instance, but to provide a special place for the practice of Christian disciplines so as to make the home churchly. The sacred things are not separated from the secular, but they are meant to be related so that all might be sacred. The ministry is a calling not to be isolated from other callings. It is a service to Christ and men, differing only in degree and not in kind from other legitimate services which Christians render. There is but *one* service in the sight of God.

We may not all be engaged in the same type of work, but we as Christians engage in whatever work we do in a common spirit. We differ greatly as human beings, in capacity, in intellectual endowment, in heredity, in background and in social situations. And each of us lives in a certain time in history and in a certain circumscribed sphere of the world's life. It is our task, as Christians, to serve Christ as Lord and Savior, with what we are and have, in the places where we find ourselves at this particular period of history. There we are to render our service, whether in terms of personal life, citizenship, parenthood, influence, example, lifework, etc. as Christians.

3. THE DECLINE OF THE SENSE OF VOCATION

This conception of man's vocation has practically lost its meaning today. Perhaps it still prevails in the professions of law, medicine, teaching and divinity. But even in these there is a secular tendency—and the ministry is not excluded.

Varied concepts

The Old Testament abounds with references to man's divine vocation in the peculiar people of God. Prophet, priest, parent, child, soldier, *et al.*, had their places in the "chosen people." The New Testament reinterprets Israel's vocation in the light of the event of Jesus Christ and the new community and life which result from that event. Early Christians remained in the world, but they were not "of" it. Paul never separates the theological and ethical aspects of the Christian faith.

Early Christianity in the Roman Empire looked with suspicion upon military service, banking, acting and the goldsmith trade.

The Middle Ages were dominated by the monastic ideal. The threefold vow of celibacy, poverty and obedience separated the clergy from domestic, economic and political life, at least in theory. The religious vocation was the true vocation. Although St. Francis sought to bring the religious vocation into the common life through his Second and Third Orders, so as to make it possible for people to share in it, he was never quite reconciled to this compromise. It was Aquinas who regarded society as a unit, in which each person and class had its place, regulations and task.

The Renaissance and the Reformation combined to break up this static society, although each movement interpreted vocationalism in a different way. The former placed great emphasis upon the choice of man in his vocation. It gave a "religious humanistic" significance to secular interests. The Reformation revolted against the aristocratic and unchristian nature of medieval society. The medieval clergy themselves became secularized; they also withdrew from society. Both the Reformation and Renaissance made room for creative individualism and renounced the double standard of vocational life.

Protestantism stressed the democratic priesthood of all believers. It emphasized the human response along with the divine initiative, and gave man a greater part in the choice of his vocation and the direction of his life. It put God in the center of *all* life. The Church was not separated from the common life. Worship became "common worship." The Word of God superseded the sacramental system, and it was given to the laity in the vernacular. The clergy married and took their places with other citizens in the community. Their obedience was to God and not to superior ecclesiastics who ruled by divine right. All clergy were on a parity before God, except for those who were designated as superintendents. God was in the midst of the common life of which the Church was the nucleus.

Protestantism had to reckon with the new spirit in the Renaissance, which interpreted man in humanistic terms according to the classical ideal of the liberal man. It had to confront rising nationalism, emerging rationalism and science, as well as political freedom. It tried to Christianize this new spirit, or at least recognize it—but Christian disunity and humanism were too strong. Men's life work became increasingly divorced from religious considerations. The doctrine of *laissez faire* was in some cases even sanctioned by Protestantism. Churches became national. Certain types of liberal theology, on the one hand, interpreted the Christian faith more in terms of experience, science and social ideals than in accordance with traditional theology. On the other hand, conservative orthodoxy tended to isolate Christianity from science and human affairs. It has been maintained that Calvinism's emphasis upon thrift sanctioned a type of individualism which ignored the community. The individual's vocation was not sufficiently related to corporate life.

The secularization of vocation

The medieval age was concerned with the purity of the saint; the Reformation was concerned with the saintliness of the common. Regardless of what we think of these two emphases, we cannot escape the fact that there has been a gradual secularization of the vocation of man until today, there are few people who conceive of vocation either in the medieval or the Reformation sense.

One of the reasons why the Nazis, Communists and Fascists have arisen is because they attempt to restore wholeness to the community and rehabilitate the place of the individual in that economy. Adherents of these social faiths have a sense of vocation. These faiths, however, are secular and vitalistic. The motives that give them birth ought to be recognized. In our vast complex industrial system, it is difficult for the individual to feel wanted or significant. The vocations of wife, husband, parent, child and family have been disintegrated. Education, likewise, has in many instances lost its power to give real "vocational" guidance to youth. Most vocational guidance is offered on the basis of social need, personal aptitude and financial returns, rather than on the basis of the will of God.

What is needed today is a renewed emphasis upon the vocation of man in the service of the living God, a recovery of the meaning of individual life in the community. Consideration, too, must be given to the basic duties and disciplines of the common man in the pursuit of his daily life and work. Christianity today must become clear on its faith, and seek to declare and implement it in such a way that the process of disintegration can not only be arrested, but that God through His Son Jesus Christ, and His empowering Spirit in the Church, may renew humanity from within through new men in Christ who live within the context of the beloved community, in the midst of the world.

The agitation which we are experiencing today is an evidence that the Holy Spirit is at work, stirring up men to inquire regarding the things that belong to their peace. The atomic bomb—that final product of our scientific age—is a serious reminder that men must learn how to live according to the purpose and power of God. Science and religion, the secular and the sacred, belong together.

The Middle Ages emphasized to excess an unworldly Christian life which warped personality and ignored the full implication of the Gospel of God. A certain type of Protestantism erred on the other side by emphasizing to excess self-sufficient individual and group interests which have proven destructive of the care of personality and of community. The solution lies in a recovery and implementation of the Biblical concept of vocation.

4. THE BASIS AND NATURE OF THE CHRISTIAN'S VOCATION

There is a definition of stewardship abroad today which is not fully Christian. It is said that man is a steward because God created and claims him. But Christian stewardship is based not only upon creation, but upon redemption. A Mohammedan could accept the definition of stewardship proposed by those who base it only upon God's creation. Man is a steward, in the Christian sense, because God's love in Christ claims him utterly. A definition of man's vocation which leaves out sin, and the place and work of Jesus Christ as Savior from its guilt and power, is deficient not only from the standpoint of the Christian faith, but deficient in the light of the exacting and tragic circumstances of real life.

Sin and vocation

The predicament of man is his loss of his true manhood, which was created by God in His own image. Through the Word of God, man is able to see his true image, and he is enabled morally to perform his vocation.

Those who face up to the Word of God are made aware of the absolute claim which God lays upon them. But our consciences tell us that we do not do what is right according to the perfect law of God. Every attempt to rationalize our way out of this predicament is only an attempt to lower the perfect will of God, or to put ourselves under the illusion that we are better than we are. Our predicament is centered not only in our moral inability but in the perverted disposition to pride and lust and appetite. There is a positive will-to-sin within us. It binds us and refuses us freedom. Every moral effort to free ourselves makes us more conscious of failure, or it may even stiffen the will-to-sin.

Our predicament is made worse by the fact that we come into a world that is already perverse. This perversity has accumulated through the centuries, and but for the restraining grace of God might have destroyed the race before now. We all partake of this social perversion. And even those who have repented of their sins and turned to God-in-Christ for truth, forgiveness and power, must confess that original sin still works in them and is prevalent in the social situations in which they live.

The redeemed vocation

This predicament is resolved only through the unmerited grace of God, revealed in the Incarnation and Cross of Christ. Here we are assured that "God was in Christ reconciling the world unto himself." This forgiveness is a miracle in the light of God's law. It does not deny the law, but through sacrificial love it offers man a new righteousness, a way for man to live a "justified" life in the face of his sinfulness and that of his world. God alone can forgive, and that through the atonement of His Son. Man's vocation is restored, *not* by a denial of his guilt, or through his moral effort, but by a divine salvation which actually enlightens and enhances his guilt but which also gives him the power to live with a new moral effort by being given a new heart and mind. Thus, the "saved" man is one who is utterly claimed by Jesus Christ. He is no longer his own; Christ is his very life, because Christ is his vocation. The vocation of the Christian rests upon the redeeming work of Jesus Christ, and the continuous sanctifying work of the Holy Spirit. Real goodness springs from that redemptive relationship, and whatever goodness the "new man in Christ" has is the work of the Spirit of God in him.

Such a conception of life does not make man unnatural, unhuman or unrealistic. In fact, the Christian is natural, human and realistic. He has no illusions about his spiritual grandeur, practices no escape mechanisms, claims no moral perfectionism. He can look at his own perversion and that of the society he inhabits without pessimism and despair. His life is one of continuous repentance and commitment. He does not think of the Christian life as a perfect life, but as a real life under God, in the concrete situation in which he finds himself. He lives in his time as a citizen of God's new order whose center of gravity is in Christ. His life in Christ is a nucleus of creativity in an evil world.

The vocation of man, then, is determined by the character and purpose of God. The secret of that purpose has been revealed by a series of divinely-initiated acts of God in history, culminating in Jesus Christ. Those who hear the Word of God and respond to it in repentance and faith are given the right to become the sons of God, not by any human power but by the power of the Spirit.

Repentance is the process whereby individuals are made capable of seeing themselves as they are in the light of God's intention for them. Through repentance they are enabled to "come to themselves."

Faith is a total surrender of the will to God. It is an identification of the self, through self-crucifixion, with God-in-Christ. Those who put their whole trust in Jesus Christ, and receive the truth and the grace he has to give, come under a "new management." They are actually a new order of men.

Many terms are used in the New Testament to describe both the objective and subjective factors in the divine salvation of man. The subjective experiences of salvation are reflections or inverted aspects of what God in Christ has done for the restoration of man to his true estate. God reveals, redeems, delivers, justifies, sanctifies, empowers, forgives, "raises from the dead," saves. Man appropriates faith and love through the power of the Spirit which accompanies the potent Word and which creates repentance.

What takes place in the man of repentance and faith is the effectual working of God's redemptive activity. Man is thus oriented toward his Creator and Redeemer; he is restored to his true manhood; he is socialized by being brought into fellowship with Christ and with kindred minds and hearts in the divine community. Man is released from the power and guilt of his sin; he is morally energized in conscience by a new, personal standard of conduct; he is enlightened in mind by the truth. His emotional capacities are released through *the* supreme loyalty.

One could go through the epistles of Paul and cite experiences in his life which illustrate the subjective aspects of God's objective revelation-activity. But always Paul gives the priority to the revelation in Jesus Christ. He is what he is by the divinely-initiated grace of God, which was manifested in history for his redemption. Paul is conscious of having been brought to his new life in Christ by a power outside himself. And he regards his Christian life as encompassing the totality of his being. Christianity, for him, had to do with every aspect of life, of history, of nature and of the universe. Jesus Christ did not take hold of one aspect of his life, but of the whole of it. For

Paul, Jesus Christ was his very life; he no longer lived; it was Christ who had "taken over." It was Paul's business to lay hold of that for which he had already been laid hold of.

The centrality of love

As H. H. Farmer puts it: The following propositions are fundamental and generally accepted by evangelical Christians as basic to any discussion of the Christian's vocation, namely, that God is love; that the full and final revelation of the fact of God's love and the way of His working have been given to men in Jesus Christ; that the revelation of the divine love in Christ gives us the standard of human relationships, a standard which men were originally created to achieve; and that it is the calling and privilege of the Christian disciple, in so far as he is truly a reconciled and forgiven person, to have increasingly in all his dealings with persons what it is not possible for unreconciled man to have, namely, the mind of Christ.[1]

No matter what different aspects God may have in His relationships with men, His love is central. The revelation of that love was costly, since God was dealing with rebellious and sinful men whose minds were blinded to the nature and purpose of God for them. The Cross has always been the central symbol of that revelation, hence love must not be thought of in sentimental terms. That love is not deserved by men. It is unmerited. And it reached man *where he is* with the power to give him the true life which God intends.

The reason why man does not find his true vocation is not because he is finite, or so closely associated with nature, or

[1] H. H. Farmer, "The Revelation in Christ and the Christian's Vocation," in *Christian Faith and the Common Life*, Vol. IV, "The Official Oxford Conference Books" (Chicago: Willett, Clark & Company, 1938), pp. 145 ff.

because God wills it. The reason is in man's choice of his own vocation apart from the purpose of God. Sin is the real predicament in man which has worked itself into the warp and woof of man's personal and corporate being. Sin is a radical perversion of man's nature from its original.

Through the Gospel, man is called to be set apart for God's purpose through the power of the Spirit in the fellowship of the Church. The effects, or fruits, of the life of the Spirit are the building up of the life of the Christian fellowship, according to the mind and heart of Christ, and the expression of the love of Christ in relationships with persons outside the Church.

Christian vocation and the world

The Christian is still related to nature. He cannot "jump out of his skin." In fact, he has a new appreciation of nature as the handiwork of God and as God's bountiful and faithful provision for the physical wants of all. No Christian is happy to see nature used for purposes contrary to the will of God, nor can he be happy to see God's good earth monopolized or abused by unholy and blasphemous people. The Christian has a new appreciation of his body, or daily bread, of clothing and shelter. A Christian ought to be a good scientist, for he possesses a new understanding of the marvels which are wrapped up in the macrocosm as well as in the microcosm. The Christian's vocation does not make him unnatural.

The Christian's vocation does not make him unhuman. He cannot isolate himself from the context of society. That would be unreal, and even pharisaical. It would deny the nature of the Christian revelation, the center of which is Jesus Christ, who took upon himself the form of man and humbled himself even unto death. Those who are "in Christ" are also in the humanity which he assumed and loved. They actually share in the social sin of the race, and bear it redemptively, as they follow Christ. Nothing human is alien to the Christian. The love that was in Christ forbids any partaker in it to assume a superior attitude toward others. Love identifies itself with even the unlovely. Only those who know their sinfulness in the light of Christ's redemptive and condescending love can really love the neighbor. Those who regard the Christian life as life "in Christ" might do well to remember that to be "in Christ" is to be in the humanity he assumed. This is the basis of the social gospel. This divine love is the bond which ties the Church together.

The Christian's vocation does not imply an idealistic perfectionism. We are called to be perfect as the Father is perfect. That is our goal. The Spirit is at work building up the people of faith into the fullness of the stature of Christ. However, this pull toward perfection does not ignore our human finitude, our sinful nature and our social perversity. We must think of perfection in terms of humility, of obedience to Christ, of love for the neighbor, and not of individual moral habits, such as the giving up of swearing, stealing, or other habits, which often lead to pride and a denial of the judgment and mercy of God. Perfection is never achieved this side of the grave. The perfection about which Christianity is concerned is the release of all that God has created man to be into its full stature in Christ. Such perfection is always tempered with repentance and faith, and is always humble and modest. It is a perfection of love and not of law.

The Christian's vocation is never complete. He "presses on toward the mark of the prize of the high calling of God in Christ Jesus." He is potentially "complete"[2] in Christ, but he works out his salvation with fear and trembling, for God is at

[2] Col. 2:10.

work in him. He continually receives his life afresh from God as he gives it up to Him daily. He grows from stage to stage in that grace and knowledge which is in Christ. The implications of the Christian's life as a steward are such that all things are to be "brought into captivity to the obedience of Christ." The sovereignty of God in Christ is totalitarian in its sweep. The task of becoming a Christian has its beginning, but it is also a process that lasts as long as life itself. The Christian is not only changed, but he is being changed. Through exposure to the Word of God, fellowship in the Christian community, the use of the means of grace, the practice of the disciplines of the Christian life, the exercise of stewardship the Christian becomes by faith fashioned into the "measure of the stature of the fullness of Christ." While Paul could say "imitate me" to his Christian comrades, he would not say that he had already apprehended the goal of his calling. He knew that there were changes taking place in his spirit and conduct under the influence of Christ, but he also knew that the source of that change was not in him. Such a conception of the Christian's vocation saves us from pride, from despair, from stagnation and from a type of self-sufficient independence that uses the grace of God for human consumption and not sanctification.

5. ASPECTS OF THE CHRISTIAN'S VOCATION

Service

The Christian is called the "salt" and the "light" of the world. His primary service is to Christ, but that service is necessarily outgoing by the very nature of Jesus Christ. "He came not to be ministered unto but to minister and give his life a ransom for many." The purpose of the Gospel is to save, that is, to produce a redeeming effect in human life. To be sure, it is its own true self first of all; but its nature is redemptive and missionary. The Christian is by nature a person animated by love-in-action. He is not only saved *from* a false life, he is also saved *for* a true life of divine mission. The two great commandments are in essence one. Love to God implied a love for the neighbor; love to neighbor is incomplete without reference to God.

As Edwin Lewis puts it:[3] A Christian interest in others is a proper issue of the life in Christ. "Because we are beneficiaries, we are also debtors." Paul felt himself a debtor to all, even though he owed them nothing. His sense of responsibility was learned from Christ who loved us, the unlovely. "The Christian is a transmitter as well as a receiver. Christ saves us through those who serve us, in order that we in our turn—the saved—may help to save others by the service that we in Christ's name may render them."[4]

The Christian, then, says Dr. Lewis, is under obligation to serve others who have played such a large part in his own life. It is through others that we have been introduced to Christ. Others make homes possible; they make possible the Church. Others make possible the framework of society which provides the conditions through which we live and come to faith in Jesus Christ. This must not be construed as a prudential doing to others what they have done to and for us. The Christian is obliged to do *more* than the Pharisees; he is to do *to* others as he would have others do to him. His relation to others is not determined by what he hopes to receive from men; it is determined by what God has done for him through others.

[3] Edwin Lewis, *The Practice of the Christian Life* (Philadelphia: Westminster Press, 1942), p. 17. This is an admirable little book, to which I owe a great deal in the preparation of this paper.

[4] *Ibid.*, p. 18.

Evangelism

The Christian is also under compulsion to *propagate the Gospel.* He must witness to his own faith by every means of communication at his disposal. The Gospel is God's and not man's. It cannot be hoarded. The Word of Life is meant for all. We have received it, and what we have received is not our own. The life in Christ cannot continue except it be given. The vocation of the Christian is that of an evangelist who is engaged in the highest human helpfulness. For one who has found his life in Christ is engaging in the highest form of human vocation when he helps another to find himself in Christ. Evangelism is not *one* form of service. It is the highest form of service which must infill every service in which the Christian engages. Evangelism is not confined to a witness of words, although such witness is essential if the witness would be complete. The Christian must bear witness with his life. He must bear his cross daily and follow Christ. His "conversation" must have about it a healing and reconciling influence. His acts must preach.

Work

The vocation of the Christian surely involves the *type of work* in which he is engaged. Christian vocational guidance involves a choice of life work which will be a form of service to God and man. And even though the Christian may be engaged in a menial task, his sense of stewardship should result in work well done, through which the Christian witness will be given. Work itself is a privilege, a gift of God. Hence, it has dignity. Through such a witness there will be injected into the world's work the saving leaven of the divine purpose. Ordinary tasks then become infused with a sacramental significance. What *is* will be brought into line with what *ought* to be.

Just how this witness may be effectively given are matters for the individual Christian to work out in harmony with the mind of Christ and local situations. It may be that there are situations from which the Christian ought to withdraw if it is against his conscience. But it may be remembered that there is no escape from the ubiquity of sin, whether in the Christian's own life, or in the situation in which he lives and works. He works, in any case, in a condition which requires constant repentance and forgiveness. By no means must the Christian regard every situation so sinful that he must engage in it in the spirit of the world, or withdraw from it in the spirit of a false perfectionism. The salt, as Dr. George A. Buttrick once said, belongs on the meat and not in the cupboard. To follow either of the above procedures is to abandon the world to its own ethos. This is a denial of the Incarnation through which the Son of God entered our sinful situation. We must live in the world whether we like it or not. To withdraw from the world will not take the world out of our hearts; nor will our consciences rest in any withdrawal from the world.

Family

The Christian's vocation involves his *family*. Its members are in a real sense his nearest neighbors. God created male and female, and He meant them to live together in complementary relationship. Sex is created of God; and, according to His intention, it is not unclean. It is sin that perverts the function of sex. It is through sex that the race is perpetuated. It is through sex relations that male and female are intimately related in a new and higher unity. When contracted through the will of God, and in the spirit of love, the married estate may become well-nigh sacramental and a means of grace through which personality is enriched, strengthened and fulfilled. Indeed, it is only "in the Lord" that man and woman may be truly joined together. The married estate is a school in which those who practice the Christian life may learn not only to live together, but learn the ways of God with men. In the Scriptures, God is the Bridegroom and Israel is his bride. The fruits of that union result in the children of God. Adultery is compared with idolatry in the Old Testament. The whole revelation of God is set within the context of the family relationship. In the New Testament, Christ is the Bridegroom and the Church the Bride. The Christian community, or the Church, is likened to a family; and in the New Testament we read of "the Church that is in thy house." The Church needs the home, and the home needs the Church; both are in need of the Gospel by which they become true to their divine functions.

The Christian's vocation inevitably involves the building of a family life in Christ, which will produce the new generation; which will become the nucleus of the Christian community, the school for the learning of Christian virtues, the channel for the communication of the Christian faith, and the pattern of God's divine order. The family will not become what God intends it to be simply because He created it as an order in the beginning; it will be redeemed to its nature and function only as the Christian faith is foundational in its structure. The state of the family in our depersonalized, industrialized, secularized and individualized environment is precarious, and it is only as its divine nature and function are understood and implemented by Christian men and women that it can become a leavening influence in Church and society.

Church

Needless to say, the vocation of the Christian involves *Churchmanship*. We are not thinking of the Church as an institution or organization. In some respects the Christian must be *against* the Church, just as he must be *against himself.* Judged by the criterion of Jesus Christ, the churches and the Christian always fall short of their high calling. They are always "becoming." Even so, with all their faults, the churches are still churches of Jesus Christ, consisting of those who have been called by God's Word and Spirit into a new relationship with Him and with one another.

It is the Christian's business to be a *Churchman,* for there is no such thing as a purely individual Christianity. Those who are "in Christ" must of necessity be in his body which is the Church. It is the Christian's concern to be actively associated with the life, work and faith of the Church. It is his responsibility to worship with his fellows in spirit and truth. Too, he must seek to purify the Church by his own practice of the Christian disciplines. He is to attend to the preaching and the teaching of the Word, and to render every assistance to the dissemination of the Gospel to the ends of the earth. He is to relate his family to the Christian community. He is to support, to the best of his financial ability, every enterprise of the Church which will do the work of Christ's body on earth. He is not only to speak a good word for the Church, but also to do good works for the sake of the Head of the Church. He is to think highly of the Church, to interest others in its Lord, and to challenge youth to enter the service of its ministries. It is his business to see to it that the Church constantly conforms to its purpose and task in the light of the revelation that gave it birth, and the Spirit that has continued it and still empowers it. He is to "see" the Church in its social function as the prophetic and critical truth-bearer, the reconciling priestly fellowship, the community of truth, worship and love. He is to seek the unity of the Church, to pray for its preservation and power, and promote its fellowship in Christ into all the areas of life. The Church, too, has its own peculiar vocation, and in the fulfillment of that destiny the individual Christian seeks to contribute as well as share.

Citizenship

The Christian's vocation involves *citizenship*. This may be accomplished individually and through groups, such as political parties, labor unions, chambers of commerce, schools, etc., with which the Christian is identified. Surely a Christian lawyer, statesman, physician, labor leader, teacher, *et al.*, can exercise a tremendous influence upon his fellows by sheer personal influence. There is a place for such leadership in our world, although we are witnessing a rising tide of group influence which is nothing short of revolutionary.

Again, the Christian is identified with *groups* in the community and nation. This is an age of groups, each concerned about special interests which affect the people who are associated with them. No Christian can unreservedly identify himself with a group which fails to take the welfare of the whole community into account. In fact, the Christian must always practice a certain detachment from every social or political group. But that he *must* participate in group thought, profession and action is quite evident. However, individual and group rights conflict, and there result competitions, struggles and even wars. These rights take many forms. The methods by which these group and individual rights seek to gain advantage vary, from attempts at persuasion to group pressures, and even violent, overt strife.

The Christian *cannot avoid* engaging in these maneuvers. There are fundamentally three points of view regarding participation in society for the sake of human welfare: (1) The position of the pacifist who will not engage in methods of violence; (2) the position of those who believe that Christian love is the divine imperative, but that it cannot be practiced in its purity in this world and therefore justify methods which will guarantee some measure of equity and justice; and (3) the position of those who insist upon the practice of love, but who will engage in active social struggle providing the cause is just. We have just gone through a controversy during the war, when advocates of these three positions presented their relation to war.

That men should will-to-live we grant. That men should exercise power we also grant. But the Christian, in the pursuit of his vocation under God, cannot avoid the imperative to practice love, or good will. The exercise of that good will must be coupled with "intelligence and good judgment." The Christian cannot be a sentimental idealist who ignores the perennial reality of conflict in society, as well as in the individual. He knows that this is a sinful world, and that all men are not Christian. He expects no spectacular social gains. He also knows that whatever he does, he does as a sinner, implicated in the sinful situation of his day. He cannot withdraw from the conflict; to do so would deny the Incarnation and his responsibility.

The Christian serves the *state* as a servant of God. "The Christian is not *also* a citizen: he *is* a Christian citizen."[5] He must be concerned about the state, for it represents the ordered framework of social life. How he serves it, whether as statesman, office holder, adviser to political leaders, or as a voter, is a matter for the Christian conscience to determine.

The Christian is under obligation to be concerned about the *community's* recreation, sanitation, housing, racial segregation

[5] Edwin Lewis, *op. cit.*, p. 119.

or injustice, prison conditions, education, liquor dispensaries, and a host of other interests.

Economic life

Christians must be concerned about the larger *economic* issues in society which individual action cannot affect. There are combinations of power and influence which influence personal life. One of these has to do with the economic order of our time. The individual often feels helpless in the face of the factory in which he works. He is a cog in the machine.

There is no easy remedy for this problem. While the Church must make studied pronouncements about social and economic justice, these statements only clarify the mind of the Church; they do not tackle the problem. The Christian, to be sure, shares the social program of the Church in its insistence upon the value of personality; the stewardship of man over the products of the earth for the benefits of all; the right of man to life, freedom, education and work; the necessity of fair wages; and a number of other rights. It is in the implementing of these principles that the Christian must exercise his vocation.

Just what method the Christian is to use in bringing about economic justice is a question which each individual will have to decide for himself. There are those who feel that the times call for some form of socialism which will still guarantee the individual rights of property, work, education and a measure of free enterprise. There are other sincere Christians who feel that a system of free enterprise alone is consistent with the Christian gospel's emphasis upon the individual. No Christian, it seems to us, can ignore both the individual and corporate emphasis of the Gospel. The Christian must participate in the economic struggle to the best of his light, again, with the full consciousness that whatever he does is not perfect because it is shot through with sinful motivation. But the only way in which a Christian can participate at all realistically in the economic struggle is in repentance and the power of the grace of God.

Race

The Christian cannot countenance *racial discrimination,* which denies the fact that Christ has "broken down the middle wall of separation" through his own broken body. Recently, the Protestant churches have renounced racial segregation as a denial of the Gospel of Christ, as a humiliation, a handicap and a burden to those who suffer it. It is devastating in its moral and spiritual effects upon majorities. It disenfranchises large numbers of our citizens politically. Churches must renounce this pattern of segregation, in all their institutions. It is the Christian faith that no race under God is superior to another; each has its right to a life of freedom of cultural development, of economic advantage, of education, of social acceptance. These principles the Christian must adopt personally and seek to promote in all his relationships.[6] The methods by which these ideals may be accomplished are varied. They surely involve the creation of public opinion, the influencing of legislation, and participation with groups in bringing about friendly relations between races. Above all, it will mean an inner conversion of a more radical nature to the truth and the love that is in Christ.

Social responsibility

In exercising his Christian vocation, the Christian must find ways and means of implementing Christian love in terms of social responsibility. He must employ a rigid sense of repentance

[6] See the official document of the section on racial tensions, adopted by the Federal Council of the Churches of Christ in America in the meeting at Columbus, Ohio in 1946. Copies are obtainable at 297 Fourth Avenue, New York City 10, New York.

toward himself and his own class, race, nation or church, in order that his judgments may not be warped by self or group interest. He must always keep alive his sense of obedience to the will of God. He must exercise his Christian citizenship as a member of the divine-human community, which is the Church. The Christian must also recognize the truth that there is no easy or over-all solution to human problems; any utopianism will result in illusion and unreal attempts at making some relative gain in social betterment in harmony with Christian love. Further, the Christian will realize that Christianity cannot be identified with any particular political or economic problem fully. And always the Christian, realizing the imperfections of his own life and in any attempt at social justice, will need the consolations of the grace of God. This should not keep him from engaging in the sinful situation, but it should give him the freedom to participate in the social struggle realistically.[7]

The late Archbishop of Canterbury, Dr. William Temple, has summed up the Christian's vocation admirably in his chapter in *Christian Faith and the Common Life*: (1) The Christian is bound to apply the standards of his religion to every departmen of his conduct. (2) In doing this, he is bound to consider the probable effects of any course of action, and choose that which in its consequences is likely to promote the greatest conformity to those standards. (3) He has the obligation because he is called to live, not by the letter of any law or precept, but by a Spirit. (4) In considering the effects of his action he must make the widest possible survey and not limit his attention to those most immediately concerned on any occasion; and especially he must consider his special responsibilities, e.g., as politician or as a man of business, or as a labor leader—the

[7] See John C. Bennett, *Christian Realism* (New York: Charles Scribner's Sons, 1941), Ch. IV.

discharge of which for him is a primary obligation. (5) Having settled his course by these principles, he must be ready to incur personal sacrifice, and to call others voluntarily to join him in sacrifice, as he follows the course chosen.

Dr. Temple continues by saying:

> And throughout he will remember, that, though he must pray for the coming of the Kingdom "in earth as it is in heaven," that hope can from the nature of the case, never be perfectly fulfilled. For that hope includes fellowship with the children of God in all generations, which cannot be realized under the ordinary conditions of mortality, and even so far as the Kingdom comes to fullness of actuality, the work has always to begin again as the generations pass and new citizens of the Kingdom are born, each infected and all infecting one another with the original sin which is self-centeredness. Consequently in this world the Kingdom is actualized always as the cross—as sacrifice, not barren indeed but also not securing the complete fulfillment of the hope for which it is made. Like our predecessors, we also, even though by God's help we win a good report on account of faith, must die without receiving the promises. Yet our strivings here have meaning for God, and they whose hearts with their treasure are in the eternal realm are those who do most to give to this temporal world the service which promotes its welfare as the ages pass and endows it with its deepest significance for eternity.[8]

6. DISCIPLINES

Christians are to grow up into the fullness of the stature that is in Christ. While one *is* Christian, in another sense he is always *becoming* a Christian. Only as we are becoming Christians do we remain Christians. The Christian life needs to be cultivated.

[8] William Temple, *op. cit.*, pp. 64-65.

The term "discipline" is unpopular in many circles. It implies a restriction upon human freedom. We have been schooled too well in the art of self-expression to take to a life of restraint. It is time we recognized the fact that everything worth while necessitates discipline. Education, art, engineering—any human pursuit—require concentration, and the elimination of interests which would disturb and confuse. The same is true of religion.

The churches have made few demands upon those who have made their profession of faith in Christ. This condition has weakened the churches and disintegrated individual Christian life. The old-fashioned disciplines of the Christian life need to be revived and interpreted. There is no way by which we automatically grow in grace and knowledge. To become a Christian requires rigid concentration, exposure to the things of Christ, and practice of the Christian life. Especially in these times do we need intellectual, religious and moral disciplines of a very exacting nature. The use of "the means of grace" —those special channels through which God makes himself known to persons of faith—is the way to spiritual growth.

The Bible

The Christian must continually steep his mind and spirit in the *Word of God.* The reading of the Scriptures provides him with a reference toward which he must continually orient himself. The Bible must be read prayerfully, expectantly and meditatively. There is a place for the study of the Scriptures, but such study must always presuppose that the Bible is God's revelation of His character, purpose, love and power. The Bible speaks to those who have ears to hear. The Christian ought to read the Bible daily, and he ought to learn to read the Bible with intelligence and for actual help in bringing his whole life into the orbit of the Biblical world view, which is centered in Jesus Christ. The Christian should expose himself to the preaching and teaching of the Word. He ought to associate himself with small groups whose purpose is to reverently study the Bible and prayerfully discuss its meaning. Since the Bible is the Word of God, it is necessary that its revelation precede prayer and worship and all other Christian activities, since it is the Bible that gives the sacraments, preaching, prayer, meditation, social action, etc., their rationale and perspective. This discipline of Bible reading needs to be restored in all churches, and the churches ought to make it a supreme concern to assist people in their daily reading of this Book.

Worship

Prayer is another discipline of the Christian life. Prayer is one of the chief means of grace. In prayer, we actually meet the living God through Christ in the Spirit in personal relationship. Prayer is the heart of the Christian life, which is communion with God. It is not primarily a means by which we bend God to our wills, but rather a discipline through which we are conformed and fixed to the purpose of God who is man's chief good. Individual Christians need to cultivate the habit and art (if it may be so called) of prayer.

Christians must not forsake the *assembling* of *themselves together for worship*. Protestantism's emphasis upon the individual's relation with God through Christ has sometimes failed to take into account adequately the necessity of the Christian's relation with the Church. Worship on the part of the corporate body of Christians is the highest form of social service rendered to God. It brings the whole human world into the presence of the God of creation and redemption and sanctification. Such worship has a powerful effect upon the individuals who worship, including the children; it also gives a strong witness to the non-Christian community; and it is the well-spring of social salvation. Any Christian who fails to associate himself with his fellows is not fully Christian. He robs himself of the tradition and the strength of the Christian community, and in time his Christian faith will become eccentric, or it may even disintegrate.

The heart of Christian worship is the *Word* and *Sacraments*. Both belong together as means of grace, although some communions have placed more emphasis upon one or the other. The Lord's Supper has ever been "the inmost sanctuary of the whole Christian worship." We have to do not with bread and wine only but with the heavenly realities which these tokens represent and seal to the worshiper. As Christians we are to feed upon the revelation which Jesus Christ has brought into our world through his broken body and shed blood. Jesus Christ and all that he means and offers is made available to those who come with repentant and believing hearts. And as Christians partake of the elements together, they are united in fellowship in him in spite of difference of background, culture, race, nationality or sex. It is difficult to imagine how a Christian can possibly regard the Lord's Supper lightly. It is embarrassing to contemplate the fact that so many Christians refuse to celebrate the Lord's Supper together, when our Lord meant it not to be a matter of controversy and division but a *fact* of unity.

Fellowship

It is difficult to overestimate the value of *Christian fellowship* even apart from worship. The Christian fellowship is itself a sacrament. It is a correcting, stimulating, therapeutic communion. The Church within the churches is one, holy, catholic and apostolic. Its unity is in its one Lord; its holiness is in its unique vocation under God; its apostolicity is in its apostolic foundations and evangelistic mission; and its catholicity is in its all-embracing and universal fellowship. The vocation of the Christian is the same: he is to be one, holy, catholic and apostolic. The Christian and the Church complement each other in the fulfillment of their vocations. The fellowship of the Church is wider than that of the local church, and its communion embraces Christians of all time past and those yet to become members of the Church.

The Christian should steep himself in the *culture of the Christian Church.* He ought to read Christian biographies, books and magazines dealing with Christian doctrine, the devotional classics of the "saints," missionary literature, and other materials which deal with the art, social action and theological discussions of the past and the present. A fund of Christian truth is found in the Church's hymnody.

Good Works

The Christian ought to engage in *Christian service.* First of all, he should witness to his faith to his neighbor, to the members of his own household, to and through the groups and agencies with which he is identified, and by means of supporting the cause of missions at home and abroad. He ought to practice stewardship in its widest ramifications. Not only ought he to give generously, but he ought to regard his money and property as gifts of God over which he is to exercise a careful stewardship. His life, his family, his capacities, his influence, his status, his time—everything he has and is—are to be administered as one who has been "bought with a price." There are many services which a Christian may render, not for the sake of merit, but as an expression of gratitude to God. It is surprising to discover how even the giving of a "cup of cold water" in the name of Christ can bring about the fruits of Christian experience. Most Christians are barren of inner richness because they do not take up their crosses daily and follow Christ. To lose life for his sake is to find it!

The common life under God

There are ways of spiritual growth which are part of *the common life*. Paul had a thorn in his flesh—some illness or impediment—which he sought God to remove. It was one of those things that come to all men. Paul was led to see it as a means of grace through which the grace of God became great in his life. Many a person who has been likewise afflicted has taken up a sickness, or a burden, and borne it to find that through it they have come to know the succor of God in an unusual way. Those who accept their daily tasks from the hand of God, and bear them in faith have entered ever deeper into the holy of holies.

In all of the disciplines of the Christian life mentioned above, it must be kept in mind that only God can bring about growth in the soul, and that only when His conditions are met. It is possible to practice certain mental and spiritual disciplines in order to bring about a "wholesome personality." With these tricks for personal development the Christian has nothing to do! Christian growth is a *by-product* of the life of repentance and faith; it is not an end which we directly seek. It is only as we lose ourselves IN CHRIST that we find ourselves. Faith is first; it is not the product of techniques. And our growth is rather a richer apprehension of the grace of God, than the addition of so much more "spirituality" to our lives.

Therefore, in Christian disciplines a rigid self-examination and self-criticism must be practiced always in the light of the Gospel of Jesus Christ, and especially of the Cross. The soul must be alone with Christ. It must also keep itself oriented toward the truth and grace that is in the central Person of the Christian faith, lest the cultivation of the spiritual life degenerate. For only Christ Jesus can really correct and guide the soul's journey. In him are all the personal elements of God and man which can save us from the subtle aberrations of some types of mysticism or secular humanism.

7. RESOURCES[9]

The resources of the Christian in the pursuit of his vocation are many, varied and adequate.

Word, Gospel and Providence

There is, first of all, the *Word of God*, of which *Jesus Christ* is the center. It is the Word that gave the Christian movement its birth, and in the ages of Christian revival has been the source of new life. It has survived the rise and fall of empires; it has been translated into many tongues without suffering loss of power to reach life with its revelation. The living Word or Act of God which first appeared in history has been faithfully recorded in the Scriptures, through which we may hear it again in our own time and tongue. And Jesus Christ is the Word's center. He holds it in unity. In him the long process of God's self-revelation came to a culmination; from him has flowed the life-giving stream for the healing of the nations. He is God's unspeakable gift to the world. He is the Gospel! He is the truth-bringer, the reconciler, the king of life and history.

[9] I am taking the liberty in this and the previous section of using some materials which I originally used in *Evangelism* and *A Call to the Churches for a Vital Evangelism*, two documents of the Department of Evangelism of the Federal Council of the Churches of Christ in America, adopted at the meeting at Columbus, Ohio in 1946.

Time only enhances his stature. There is no resource like unto Jesus Christ and the Book which testifies to him.

The Christian has a resource in the *Gospel*, that is, the full sweep of the whole revelation of God. This Good News is still news! Perhaps we have heard it so often that it has lost its novelty and wonder. But that God created the world in love, and that through His Son He has visited us with reconciling mercy, so that we might have new life, is the miracle of miracles. Through the Holy Spirit this salvation is made efficacious. The whole Gospel, centering in the life, teachings, death, resurrection, ascension, reign and coming again of Jesus Christ as Lord is relevant to every human situation. It takes man's sin and guilt realistically; it takes his moral inability seriously; and it takes his predicament seriously. The Gospel is glorious, adequate, comprehensive, complete. In its essence and its effectiveness it proves itself! There is but one Gospel, and it is the only resource, basically, of the Christian and of the Church. There is no other Gospel.

Another resource is the *Providence of God*. Today men are frankly afraid. Some regard it as impossible to believe in Providence; they offer a counsel of despair in the light of the atomic bomb. However, the Christian believes that God has created and still upholds His world. The ultimate purpose of God cannot be thwarted, even though man takes his own life individually or collectively. God is not surprised by what man does. Our faith in the forgiveness of sins and in the resurrection of the dead at God's hand gives us the assurance that whatever happens, God will not only be vindicated in His justice, power and love, but that believers will have their temporal lives swallowed up of eternity and taken into a new existence, which will be the fulfillment and consummation of what through grace was begun here on earth. We cannot hope to describe what that future will be like, but we are assured that it will be God's and be shared by those "who are called according to his purpose." The purpose of God is eternal. It undergirds all things. It will eventually be vindicated. Without that, we would lapse into futility and nothingness. With it all things turn out for good.

The Church

The *Church* is a great resource for the Christian, more precious and meaningful now that it has been re-formed in many respects through suffering. The Church is no longer regarded as a product of men, or even as an aggregation of Christians who make it, but as the creation of God and as integral to the Gospel. God alone through His Son and the Spirit creates the Church. Though the outer forms of the churches may change, and though there may be division in the Church and unworthy members in these churches, God is at work in these churches and in Christians in a redeeming way. The individual Christian needs the Church, and the Church needs the individual. We take heart in the fact that the Church stands as a testimony to the power and authority of Christ and the Holy Spirit.

We think not only of the *Church* in our times, but of the Church throughout its life *in history*. While we cannot take any ultimate assurance from the past, since we face a new and unique situation, we can nevertheless take courage in the historical fact that God did deliver His people in times of dire distress, and in days of severe persecution. And what shall we say of the Church's missionary enterprise? And of the reality of the ecumenical Church in this day of international confusion? The Christian community exists and survies; it testifies to its divine origin and protection, and to its unique reality as the true fellowship among men in Christ. It is the symbol of a redeemed humanity through the power of the living Gospel. The Church is an infinite potential for the redemption of mankind.

There are many resources upon which the Christian may lean in a time like this. Christian *literature* today is rich in content and alive in its presentation. There is a *revival of interest in religious affairs today* which is prompted by the tragic times in which we live. Who can doubt that the Spirit of God is moving men to inquire about the profound realities of existence? There is a *revival of theology* abroad, which calls us back to the Biblical sources of the faith, to discover afresh the living content of divine revelation. All churches are not only concerned about *evangelism* today, but they are actually engaged in studies and campaigns to reach men effectively with the Gospel of Jesus Christ. Various *sects* and *cults* which attract millions are a rather embarrassing evidence of the hunger of people for a supernatural religion which is definite, experiential and which issues in warm fellowship.

Is it not encouraging to note that the great *scientists* of our times are anxious men, and that they have come to the conclusion that only a new quality of character offers any protection for the most part against the adverse use of atomic energy? There is a *spirit of inquiry* abroad, generated, we believe, by the Spirit of God. And this spirit of inquiry is liveliest in this generation of youth, who have been the victims of war. These *youths* represent a potential reservoir of power and influence, for good or ill.

There are *means of communication* today which are not evil in themselves. They represent quicker, more effective and dramatic ways of communicating the Gospel.

There is a greater desire on the part of *Christians to work together* for common ends. This is an encouraging sign.

And last, and not least, is our own Christian *experience of grace* and *prayer*. The apostle Paul continually built upon his *past experience with Christ*. He believed that what God had begun He would finish. He was assured on the basis of what God had done, that He would continue to act. Paul's assurance of God's faithfulness was a resource which gave him power to face and endure all things. Together with this experience of grace there is *prayer*. More things are wrought by prayer than this world dreams of, it has been said. Perhaps, when we reach the end of life's pilgrimage, we shall discover that prayer has been God's choicest gift to man, for through it we have fellowship with the living God, a fellowship in which we truly achieve our Christian vocation as children of God.

Further Reading for Section III

Barry, F. R. *What Has Christianity to Say?* New York: Harper & Brothers, 1938.

Bell, Bernard I. *Religion for Living*. New York: Harper & Brothers, 1940.

Bennett, John C. *Christian Realism*. New York: Charles Scribner's Sons, 1941.

———. *Christianity and Our World*. New York: Association Press, 1937.

Bruner, Emil. *The Divine Imperative*. New York: The Macmillan Company, 1942.

———. *Justice and the Social Order*. New York: Harper & Brothers, 1946.

Calhoun, Robert L. *God and the Common Life*. New York: Charles Scribner's Sons, 1935.

Harkness, Georgia. *Religious Living*. New York: Association Press, 1937.

JOHNSON, F. ERNEST. *The Social Gospel Re-examined.* New York: Harper & Brothers, 1940.

KELLEY, THOMAS R. *A Testament of Devotion.* New York: Harper & Brothers, 1941.

LEWIS, EDWIN. *The Practice of the Christian Life.* Philadelphia: Westminster Press, 1942.

NIEBUHR, REINHOLD. *An Interpretation of Christian Ethics.* New York: Harper & Brothers, 1935.

STEERE, DOUGLAS. *Prayer and Worship.* New York: Association Press, 1938.

VISSER 'T HOOFT, W. A. and OLDHAM, J. H. *The Church and Its Function in Society.* Chicago: Willett, Clark & Company, 1937.

VLASTOS, GREGORY and SCOTT, R. B. Y. *Towards a Christian Revolution.* Chicago: Willett, Clark & Company.

"The Official Oxford Conference Books":

Volume IV, *Christian Faith and the Common Life.* Chicago: Willett, Clark & Company, 1938.

Oxford Conference, Official Report. J. H. Oldham, ed. Chicago: Willett, Clark & Company, 1938.

SUBJECTS AND MEMBERSHIP OF THE COMMISSIONS

COMMISSION I-A

VOLUME I. *The Challenge of Our Culture*

CLARENCE T. CRAIG: *Chairman*
JAMES LUTHER ADAMS
ELMER J. F. ARNDT
JOHN K. BENTON
CONRAD BERGENDOFF
BUELL G. GALLAGHER
H. C. GOERNER
GEORGIA HARKNESS
JOSEPH HAROUTUNIAN
WALTER M. HORTON
JAMES H. NICHOLS
VICTOR OBENHAUS
WILHELM PAUCK
ROLLAND W. SCHLOERB
EDMUND D. SOPER
ERNEST F. TITTLE
AMOS N. WILDER
DANIEL D. WILLIAMS

COMMISSION I-B

VOLUME II. *The Church and Organized Movements*

The Pacific Coast Theological Group:

RANDOLPH CRUMP MILLER: *Chairman*
JAMES C. BAKER
EUGENE BLAKE
KARL MORGAN BLOCK
JOHN WICK BOWMAN
ELLIOTT VAN N. DILLER
GALEN FISHER
ROBERT M. FITCH
BUELL G. GALLAGHER
CYRIL GLOYN
GEORGE HEDLEY

JOHN KRUMM
MORGAN ODELL
PIERSON PARKER
CLARENCE REIDENBACH
JOHN SKOGLUND
DWIGHT SMITH
FREDERIC SPIEGELBERG
EVERETT THOMSON
ELTON TRUEBLOOD
AARON UNGERSMA
HUGH VERNON WHITE
LYNN T. WHITE
GEORGE WILLIAMS

Guests of the Theological Group:

JOHN H. BALLARD
THEODORE H. GREENE
EDWARD OHRENSTEIN
EDWARD L. PARSONS
HOWARD THURMAN
STACY WARBURTON
FREDERICK WEST

COMMISSION II

VOLUME III. *The Gospel, The Church and The World*

KENNETH SCOTT LATOURETTE: *Chairman*
EARL BALLOU
JOHN C. BENNETT
NELS F. S. FERRÉ
JOSEPH FLETCHER
HERBERT GEZORK
EDWARD R. HARDY, JR.
ELMER HOMRIGHAUSEN
STANLEY HOPPER
JOHN KNOX
BENJAMIN MAYS
WILLIAM STUART NELSON
RICHARD NIEBUHR
JUSTIN NIXON
NORMAN PITTENGER
JAMES McD. RICHARDS
LUMAN J. SHAFER
PAUL SCHERER
WYATT A. SMART
GEORGE F. THOMAS
FRANK WILSON

COMMISSION III

VOLUME IV. *Toward World-Wide Christianity*

O. FREDERICK NOLDE: *Chairman*
EDWIN R. AUBREY
ROSWELL P. BARNES
JOHN C. BENNETT

Arlo A. Brown
E. Fay Campbell
J. W. Decker
H. Paul Douglass
Charles Iglehart
F. Ernest Johnson
Charles T. Leber
Henry Smith Leiper
John A. Mackay
Elmore N. McKee
Lawrence Rose
Stanley Rycroft
Matthew Spinka
A. L. Warnshuis
A. R. Wentz
Alexander C. Zabriskie

Volume V. *What Must the Church Do?*

Henry P. Van Dusen

Date Due

4-15			
11-13			
JAN 2 '57			
JAN 19 '61			
MAR 31 '64			
SEP 29 '65			
APR 15 '66			
MAY 4 '66			
MAR 7 '69			
FEB 5 '75			
OCT 3 '77			
DEC 2 '77			
DEC 16 '77			
NOV 28 '78			